Living Beyond the Hurt

Kimberly McCall

Copyright © 2023 Kimberly McCall

All rights reserved.

Cover art done by author.

ISBN: 979-8-9868350-0-6

Scripture quotations marked KJV are from the King James Version of the Bible.

Scripture quotations marked NKJV are from the New King James Version Copyright © 1982 by Thomas Nelson. Used by permission. All rights reserved.

Scripture quotations marked ESV are from are from The ESV® Bible (The Holy Bible, English Standard Version®), copyright © 2001 by Crossway, a publishing ministry of Good News Publishers. Used by permission. All rights reserved.

Dedicated to all of those who read the very rough first drafts. Your time will forever be appreciated.

4

Contents

Forward	5
Chapter One	7
Chapter Two	15
Chapter Three	23
Chapter Four	32
Chapter Five	43
Chapter Six	56
Chapter Seven	64
Chapter Eight	71
Chapter Nine	84
Chapter Ten	94
Chapter Eleven	101
Chapter Twelve	107
Chapter Thirteen	112
Chapter Fourteen	123
Chapter Fifteen	134
Chapter Sixteen	140
Chapter Seventeen	146

Forward

I wrote most of this book in ten days.

Ten days after a life-altering event occurred. Most of that portion has been unchanged. It's been edited and spell-checked, but the content remains the same. It flows from my raw emotions following that event: confusion, anger, bitterness, frustration, sadness, anxiety, peace, understanding, and restoration.

But before we get into the details of the event... before this book begins and my story begins to unfold... I want to give you a warning.

You may have picked this book up, read the summary, and decided that you have found yourself in the same situation. You were once (or maybe still are) fearful, intimidated, ashamed, broken, or perhaps just lacking the feeling of being loved.

Maybe you, too, grew up in an environment where it was more likely that you would be hit than hugged. A place more likely for you to be screamed at than to hear the words "I love you." Maybe someone did something to you that still holds you in its grip today. Perhaps you were the one who failed the responsibilities to yourself or someone under your care and still can't shake the guilt all these years later. Or maybe you don't find yourself relating to any of it but want to help those who do.

No matter why you decided to read this book, I hope it helps you in whatever way it can. If you're searching for peace, I hope you find peace. If you have questions, I hope you find answers. If this serves to be a step on your way to restoration, I hope it helps you on your journey.

But just keep in mind that this book alone cannot fix all of your problems. It can motivate you to fix them. It can help you realize that the things you experienced were never your fault. It can point out destructive behaviors that you have adopted as a way to cope. These lessons I learned the hard way can help you. Seeing my journey to healing can show you that you're not stuck where you are. Reading this can help you realize that you aren't alone in your struggle.

6

It can do all of those things for you… but one thing it will not do is give you the radical transformation that you may be looking for. For that, I point you to the only Words that matter. Yes, read my book for inspiration. Read it for comfort. Read it for a realization. Read it to build your faith.

But only He can give you transformation.
Before, during, and after you finish reading this book,
spend some time with His words.
Dwell in His presence.

Because only in Jesus are:
Old things made new.
Broken things made whole.
Dead things brought to life.

* Reader's Note: anyone mentioned in this book (aside from Harrison) will not be mentioned by their real name for privacy reasons. I will refer to any other person as a random initial… for example, a friend might be called "K" or "C" to ensure anonymity.

CHAPTER ONE:
Unmasking My Brokenness

*"We are hard-pressed on every side, **yet not crushed;** we are
perplexed, **but not in despair;**
persecuted, **but not forsaken;** struck down, **but not
destroyed..."***
— 2 Corinthians 4:8-10 (NKJV)

"I was born into darkness.
Seemingly doomed from the start."

That is an excerpt from the journal of my fourteen-year-old
self. A little dramatic... a lot melancholy... that's always been my
style. Especially when I was a moody teenager.

But that statement... however dramatic or theatrical... was
how I truly felt at the time. I sincerely believed that there was no
light at the end of the tunnel for me. I thought my life was doomed
before I was given a chance... before I even existed.

My mother and father rushed into a quick marriage the day
after my mother turned eighteen. She was willing to do whatever it
took to get out of her house. The irony is that I would find myself
in the same place when I turned eighteen. However, when you
study the topic of abuse, and you look deeper into the story, you'll
realize that it's more than just irony. It's the continuation of a cycle
-- a cycle that plagued her family for generations and my father's
as well.

My parents didn't *really* know each other. They didn't date
long before jumping into marriage. A little less than a year later,
they were welcoming their first child into the world. Their world.
Their *already dysfunctional* world.

I imagine that it must have been hard... being a married
couple with a baby at nineteen and twenty-two. My mother has
never worked; my dad carried the weight of the finances on his
shoulders. I can't imagine the stress he would have been under
when, still, under the age of twenty-five, another child would be
born.

That child would be me.

Stressed out, facing the harsh world with little family support... he probably felt like his world was crumbling. Stress and bills were piling up, and resources were quickly running out. Being stuck with the sole burden of having to provide for a growing family (eventually, there would be five of us).

I imagine that must have been hard.
I know that it had to have been hard.

I don't remember a lot from when I was a child. I do know that I did have a "normal life" somewhere at the start. I have vague memories of life when my parents seemed to want to be parents. They've never been perfect... as no parents are... but things shifted at some point during our timeline.

The shift from normal to nightmare happened early. I don't remember being tucked in at night and having a bedtime story read to me. There never was a prayer time with my parents praying over me. Sparing a few seldom moments, I don't remember experiencing the little things that make childhood memories so fond.

My dad had a stable job working in a grocery store. I remember when he was still working primarily because of a traumatic experience linked to it. One day... while I was still really young... I decided to shove a tiny doll shoe up my nose because I wanted to know what it smelled like. I was a curious child with a big imagination... at least... that's what I've been told by my Nana countless times.

And my curious mind, with my big imagination, *really* wanted to know what a doll shoe would smell like. I figured the best way to do that was to fit it in my nostril if I even could. It looked small. It could totally fit into my nostril.

And it did.
A little too well.

I remember running into the other room screaming. I thought I was going to die. There was no way I could survive with a rubbery doll shoe stuck in my nose for the rest of my life. I was screaming. My mother started screaming. The cat, Snowbelle, was looking at us as if we had lost our last brain cells.

It was pure chaos.

I love my mother, but she's never been good at handling stressful situations. The only thing she could think to do was call my dad at work. She told him he needed to come home immediately and get the doll shoe out of my nose.

He came home in a rush and a huff. He questioned why I would ever stick a doll shoe in my nose. My answer made him laugh, and he warned me that curiosity killed the cat before he eventually got the shoe out of my nose.

I love this memory because it reminds me that both of my parents did care for me; they just weren't sure how to show it.

My mother has never handled strong emotions well. No one ever really taught her how to deal with them. On the opposite end of the spectrum, my dad was taught unhealthy ways to cope with strong emotions. Through observational learning, he was taught that you handle strong emotions with alcohol or violence. Sometimes both. Often both.

As a result, I felt neglected most of my life.
Like a burden.
Unlovable.

My parent's marriage was riddled with dysfunction. Affair after affair. Some abuse. Constant screaming. Belittling any attempt of the other to do something outside their comfort zone. Continuous jealousy. Both sides were equally guilty. Neither side was in the right.

What didn't help was that we lived in a small apartment. It was too small for the five of us: me, my mom, my dad, my older sister, and the friend of my parents that lived with us. So I heard everything. All day. All night.

Although... where the apartment lacked space, it made up for in quality. It was a pretty good apartment from the few memories I have of it. *Especially* given the budget my parents had.

Fitting the theme of my life, our apartment caught on fire one night. I don't exactly remember how it started, but the image of standing in front of it as the firefighters tried to put out the fire is forever seared into my brain. I can remember the neighbors standing around us... some were trying to comfort us. Some were just there out of morbid curiosity.

After the fire, we started hopping around. We never stayed anywhere for too long. From kindergarten until halfway through sixth grade, I moved every year... sometimes multiple times a year. I often wonder if the fire had something to do with it; maybe they feared that if they stayed somewhere too long, it would be ruined. I never figured out the real answer.

I also never attempted to make friends because -- in my mind -- there was no point. I would be leaving almost as quickly as I started the school anyway. I went as far as no longer announcing that I was moving. I didn't like the awkwardness that the last day before a move brought. I didn't like saying goodbye. I didn't like the other kids treating me so awkwardly. I didn't like the production that teachers would make out of it.

I would simply disappear, and the teacher
(I assume — I obviously wasn't there)
would have to announce that I moved schools.

Move after move, the quality of the places we stayed diminished. A life that began in a nice apartment slowly made its way into a trailer park full of sketchy people. And another one. And then another. An occasional house for a couple of months. Followed by a couple more sketchy trailer parks... finally landing in what seemed to be a good house. By that point, my family of four (plus one) had become a group of eight with an addition of three new sisters.

The only problem was that the lady renting it to us did not care to fix anything. She would even go as far as finding a way to blame it on us most of the time. If a dishwasher broke down due to being old, we somehow broke it.

We once had to live in a motel room for a couple of weeks after her son tore the linoleum trying (for the first time since we moved there) to fix a floor problem. She blamed us for the tear and started the eviction process.

As a result, all eight of us stayed in a small room... all eight of us. Three adults. Five children... the youngest two being autistic. Crammed together with only one bathroom, two beds, and one tiny desk chair. I wasn't privileged enough to sit alone on the chair, so I was always forced to squeeze onto the bed or sit on the floor. Most often, I found myself sitting on the floor. All we had to eat was whatever people brought us because all our money was spent on the cost of the room.

Eventually, our landlady calmed down and allowed us to move back in. But after that... my parents never asked her to fix or replace anything else. From that point... everything in the house crumbled.

I looked up one day and realized
I was living in a tattered house.
Fitting — a tattered house for a tattered soul.

As a kid, the house you live in plays a much more significant role than it seems. When I was younger, I was scared to invite anyone over. There were a particular group of girls in my school who would make fun of you if you were on the poorer side... and that's where I always found myself.

My theory was... if no one ever saw my house... they wouldn't see how poor I was. I tried to disguise how little money my parents had. I took great care of any clothes, shoes, and accessories I was given. I was in denial. I refused to acknowledge the truth.

I didn't want to admit that I was the kid living in a home where you had to use pliers to turn on the water. Where there were tears throughout the linoleum floors. Where the hot water wasn't hot for long.

A house where there were holes in the wall and doors. That we had a bathtub that never looked clean no matter how long you would scrub it and a toilet to match. Mildew on the curtains. Mold on the ceiling. Deep cracks in the brick outside.

Tattered...but not shattered.

Tattered means to be in poor condition,
but shattered means to be damaged or *destroyed*.

Tattered things can be patched up, as we see with clothing. Tattered things can be restored. Tattered things can be fixed, but this isn't the same for things that have been shattered. Shattered things are broken beyond repair.

When talking to Harrison, my husband, about this, he said, "When I think tattered, I imagine a cloth full of tears and scrapes... but nothing that can't be sown. When I think shattered, I see broken glass that can't go back the same way."

He went on to write an excerpt for this book:

Tattered but not shattered
Battered but not beaten
Bruised but not buried
Damaged but not destroyed

Even though I didn't know it at the time, that's where I was. My victory over everything I was facing was already won. It was won a long time ago on a cross. As damaged as I thought I was, I wasn't destroyed. I wasn't demolished. Even shattered things... things in our human definition that can't be fixed... can be mended together in the Potter's hand.

But... the thing is... I wasn't actually shattered.
I was on the route to wholeness.

The environment I lived in was in poor condition, but the houses or apartments were always still functional. It didn't look the best, but it worked. And the same went for me. I was tattered. Worn out from being beaten down by the waves of this life. But I wasn't shattered as I had thought. I wasn't destroyed. God made sure of that; there was still hope.

This darkness that seemed to hover over my life started before I was born... the result of a few thoughtless and very reckless choices. It weighed heavily on me. I was born into dysfunction, and dysfunction was all that I knew.

Until God.

This is my story of the restoration that I never thought possible. A story of learning to forgive the "unforgivable." A story of finding strength where I felt weakest. But most of all, this story is a reminder that if God can do it for me... He can do it for you. What He's done once, He can do again.

You can find hope in the middle of your hopelessness.
You can find peace in the storm.
You can find joy in the darkness.
You can find strength when you're worn.

Keep in mind as you read these pages that your story may not be my story, but He's fighting for you too. He's writing your story too. He can use the messes we deem "unusable." You may not relate to everything I've been through, but He's your hope just as He has been mine my whole life long.

Remember, we're all on a route to wholeness --
let Him guide you along the way.

I'm going to tell my story and a few lessons I learned along the way. I pray that this book gives you the encouragement that pain isn't permanent. I pray that this shows you that there is always hope in the valley.

Even when we can't see it for ourselves.

"Surely goodness and mercy shall follow me all the days of my life,
***and I shall dwell in the house of the Lord forever.*"*
Psalm 23:6 (ESV)

CHAPTER TWO:
You Can't Fool God

"The LORD is near to the brokenhearted
and saves the crushed in spirit."
— Psalm 34:18 (ESV)

As we've already established... I don't remember a lot from my childhood. I have very few good memories... most of which have been tainted.

For example, a memory I love was when our next-door neighbor gave my older sister and me a Barbie mansion that their granddaughter no longer used. Along with the dollhouse was a bag FULL of dolls. Not only dolls but doll *clothes*.

I don't know if this paints the picture of how poor we were, but all of my barbies had no clothes and matted hair. They were always hand-me-downs that lost their quality long before they got into my hands. We *never* had a closet full of clothes for our Barbies. I was amazed by the outfits I could put together for each doll. I honestly think this is where my love for fashion started.

This wonderful gift was given to us around Christmas time. They were probably making room for the new toys they would give their grandchildren and decided to give the old toys to the neighborhood kids who ran around in ratty clothes and had wild, unbrushed hair.

To them, it was probably a form of charity...
to us, it was a blessing we would never forget.

We didn't get many presents that year. Seeing the Barbie mansion was like a dream come true, even if it was a little broken. Being able to dress up those dolls in whatever outfits I felt like putting together was so exciting.

Seems like a good memory, right?

Shortly after we received that gift, it vanished. Gone without a trace. This is something that would go on to happen a lot more later in my life. When I would be gifted anything of value, it would be sold before I had the chance to notice that it was gone. The goal was to get money that my parents could spend irresponsibly.

I learned to deal with this, but I always figured that things of sentimental value were off-limits for them. An unspoken rule. I never expected that anything I was emotionally attached to would be sold behind my back.

But as I would grow to learn, there was nothing that was off limits to them. This selling gifts behind my back wasn't just limited to gifts from friends or neighbors; this happened with gifts from family as well.

For context, I was obsessed with becoming a photographer growing up. It's kind of funny that I ended up marrying one. I was convinced I would become a world-famous wildlife photographer at the time. I loved taking pictures of the outdoors... mushrooms specifically for some reason. I think that everyone goes through the phase of wanting to be a photographer, and my phase lasted until I was sixteen.

For my birthday that year, all I wanted was a camera. I knew that a higher-end digital camera was impossible because $200-$300 was way out of the price range for anyone who wanted to buy me a present. I settled for a $50 camera that would instantly print a picture. I was elated to receive it. I couldn't download any pictures to my phone, but it was a chance to gain practice.

My older sister bought me a white version of that camera and brought it to my party at the church (thrown by my now mother-in-law). Not only was it a gift from my sister (who was married, no longer lived with us, and I never got to see), it was a gift for my sixteenth birthday — so it had an extra sense of sentimental value. To my dismay, this gift was not exempt from being sold.

As I got ready for school one day, I snapped a picture of my dog next to my relatively new journaling Bible. My two loves — Jesus and my dog — all in one picture. I thought it would be a funny caption and decided I would take a picture of that picture and post it later.

That was the last picture I was able to take with that camera. When I got home, it was missing, and no one could provide an answer for where it could have gone. It may sound a little dramatic, but I cried for an hour afterward. To me, it was the last straw. I knew that they neither respected me nor cared about hurting my feelings.

After that, I gave up my photography aspirations. There was now a dark cloud looming over that profession. Being a photographer was yet another dream sunk by a tainted memory. Another dream that would be used to mock me. What chance would I have to become a photographer? They made sure to explain all of the ways I wouldn't be able to make it.

* * *

My psychology professors would go on to explain my abnormal lack of memories during my childhood as 30% normal and 70% repressed memories. Some schools of thought in psychology deem repressing memories as impossible, so not all of them would agree on the specifics.

It would be abnormal if I remembered *everything* from my childhood — it's completely normal to forget a few memories here and there. This is why photographs are so important; they can help jog memories. So couple the normal process of forgetting memories with the trauma I endured, and the result is that I have very few memories of my childhood before I was twelve.

It doesn't help that I also have little to no pictures of my childhood to jog my memory. My parents have never been the sentimental type... at least not with me. Keeping up with pictures between our many moves was not a priority for them. There was no putting my art on the refrigerator door; I remember many times when I put my own art up just to find them in the trash later. No saving grades that I was super proud of. No box full of pictures, drawings, and report cards.

These are things that I saw other parents doing for their children. My classmates had a box or a scrapbook for their school memories. Some of them already had an almost full box. I couldn't accept that I didn't have one, so I decided that I had to make one for myself. When I was still in elementary school, I started my own box. Except, it wasn't a box per se... more like a memory folder as I didn't have access to a cute box.

I kept every award I received in this folder. I kept them to remind myself that no matter how many times they would call me stupid, I was not stupid. I held on to them as reminders that I wasn't actually worthless.

My memory folder was discovered a few times, and I was relentlessly made fun of for it. I was called prideful and had to save my precious memory folder from destruction multiple times. No one seemed to be mindful of the underlying factor: I didn't just keep the folder for the reasons they labeled as prideful. I just wanted to feel like they cared. I wanted them to find it and thank me for keeping up with all those memories because they had forgotten to save them. I wanted them to be happy to find it, not offended.

This has been a recurring theme throughout my entire life. I just wanted to be loved by someone. Anyone. My whole life, I have always felt like the outcast or black sheep of my family. Everyone else seemed to get along so well. They liked the same things. They enjoyed going places that I didn't have fun at. They liked to watch movies that I didn't want to watch. They all seemed to fit perfectly together -- like puzzle pieces.

Many days, my family would be gathered around the television watching a movie together while I was hidden away in my room... terrified to leave. I was afraid that if I did, more abuse would be waiting outside my door. My biggest worry was that a string of insults was already loaded in their slingshot... ready to fire the moment I stepped out the doorway.

Insults always led me to be defensive, or it would lead me to be a crying mess. With either response, this would fuel the fire... leading to much worse. Because of this, I learned to hide my emotions. I learned to shut down my emotions so no one else could see them.

I've always joked that I would be a good actress because I learned to mask my genuine emotions and produce fake ones (if needed) in order to survive as a kid. I was good at it. I learned their patterns of behavior and used that knowledge against them.

A *response* gave them *ammunition*, so I stopped giving them a response. That would kill their fun. Instead of reacting in front of them, I would react later in privacy. Eventually, I stopped expressing emotion in public altogether. Rage would build up inside me, threatening to erupt at any moment. Sadness would sink my spirit lower and lower. My strong emotions would be pushed down until I felt nothing at all.

Feeling no emotion is not normal.
Or healthy.

While this was only a coping mechanism that worked in *this specific situation*, I started applying it to all other situations. It became very unhealthy. This led me to start building walls between myself and everyone attempting to get close. The minute someone tried to show that they cared, I would do something... anything... to push them away.

This was yet another very harmful trauma response. I was convinced that if I never let anyone close, there was no way I would be betrayed again. If I didn't have any expectations, I would never be disappointed.

I even found myself trying to build a wall between myself and God. I would approach Him as if He were a distant God. If you're struggling with that too, I want to assure you that He is not distant (Jeremiah 23:23). However, I would try to mask my real feelings... convinced that I could fool God. If I approached Him like He were distant, maybe He wouldn't notice anything.

I could at least pretend that He didn't.

You can't fool the One that knows the exact amount of strands of hair on your head (Luke 12:7). You can't fool the One who saw your unformed substance (Psalm 139:16). You can't trick

God because God knows you. The real you. He sees you (Genesis 16:13). The real you.

And that's the beauty of it all. He sees the me that I may not show anyone else... and He still loves me with all of my faults and failures. *Despite* my faults and failures. I can never get over the fact that God saw me in my worst condition and didn't discard me as everyone else did.

Putting up a wall between God and me only delayed my healing. God can't work on things I don't allow Him to. He can't mend the pieces I won't offer to Him. That's the point of free will; God is a gentleman who will not force us to do anything.

He won't make you walk down the road to healing, but He will nudge you to do so. And if you choose to walk that road, He'll hold your hand along the way. At the end of the day, it is your choice and your choice alone.

Acting like I was okay to God and everyone else did no good for me. It only ended up making me feel more alone. Never allowing anyone in only left me feeling more hopeless. It's okay to not be okay, but God won't leave you that way if you let Him.

God was with Ezekiel — even when Ezekiel was in captivity by the river of Chebar (Ezekiel 1:1-3). Your circumstance or location does not hide you from Him. His love can reach you right where you are.

Wherever you are.
No matter how you feel.

You are not hidden from Him (Psalm 139:15).
Captivity did not hide Ezekiel from God.
He's with us during the good and the bad.

"And the hand of the Lord was upon him there."
Ezekiel 1:3 (ESV)

He sees you. Think of how powerful that statement really is. Don't try to hide behind a mask. Be open and honest with God. Express your true feelings. Expose all of your pain. Unmask your brokenness.

My pastor (who also happens to be my father-in-law) once taught a series called "Boundaries For Your Soul." In the second lesson of this series, he talked about brokenness. He discussed a few ideas that have always stuck with me.

He said (and I'm paraphrasing), "you need to expose your brokenness to God, so the enemy doesn't exploit it." He went on to explain that being broken is not a sin, but sin will take advantage of the brokenness in your spirit, as it did with Cain in Genesis 4.

"A merry heart does good, like medicine,
but a broken spirit dries the bones."
Proverbs 17:22 (NKJV)

Masking my true emotions became a trauma response for me... and Harrison quickly caught on to this. I never seemed to cry around others. I never seemed to get angry at others. I showed little emotion around other people and never seemed to react in the moment.

After four years into our relationship, I was crying in the car after the death of a family member. He looked over at me and told me he was proud of me. Just so you can get a picture... I'm in the crying mess response... not the defensive response. Tears are streaming down my cheeks. My hair is messy from constantly pushing it out of my face. Snot is going everywhere, and I can't even help it. A mess. That is what I looked like.

You can understand my confusion about why he would be proud of me. Especially given the circumstances of that weekend. After questioning his sanity, he responded with something along the lines of, "a couple of years ago, you weren't even able to cry around me." He told me that I was cracking. My hard, rough exterior that I was so proud of... that took me so long to build. It was cracking.

That's when I realized how far I had come. And I have to thank God for that. He worked in ways I didn't think possible. When I placed my brokenness in His hands and stopped trying to control it all myself, mountains of pressure were lifted off my shoulders. Releasing all that resentment, bitterness, and confusion into God's hands was the best decision I could have made.

Expose your brokenness to God. You don't have to play pretend with the Lover of your soul. You don't have to act like you have it all together with the One who saves us.

Be open.
Be honest.

I believe that some of the most authentic worship we engage in is allowing ourselves to be broken before God. Acknowledging His sovereignty and allowing ourselves to be vulnerable before Him, not putting on a front of a (fake) perfect life. Showing trust in His character and ability to deliver us.

He sees you.
The real you...
and He loves you all the same.
You are not hidden from Him (Hebrews 4:13).
Isn't that wonderful?

CHAPTER THREE:
You Aren't Unlovable

*"The LORD hath appeared of old unto me, saying, **Yea, I
have loved thee with an everlasting love**: therefore with
lovingkindness
have I drawn thee."*
— Jeremiah 31:3 (KJV)

My earliest memory is being dropped by my uncle.
Although, he wasn't really my uncle. I'm still not sure exactly how
we were related, but we called him uncle for the sake of simplicity.
I have a vague memory of this experience, and I'm not sure if I
should even be able to remember it.

I remember that he decided to pick me up and throw me in
the air... above concrete. Not the brightest idea. I'm sure he
planned to catch me, but he missed. Of course. I then come
crashing down at full speed. Harrison (my husband) and I are
pretty sure this is why I am so terrified of heights to this day.

Considering this is my earliest memory,
it seems like things could only go up from there.
I assure you — they do not.

My next memory is one that I didn't even know that I
remembered until my sister brought it up a couple of years ago.
Then everything came rushing back to me. I pushed my older sister
out of our trailer door with no porch attached to it. It was the day
(or a couple of days after) we moved into it.

In my defense, she stole my toy *and* terrorized me about it.
She kept whining about wanting to go outside, and I didn't know
there wasn't a raised porch area attached to the back door... so...
little me pushed her. It was partly to be helpful because if I made
her go outside, she couldn't get in trouble. I also wanted an excuse
to push her since she stole my toy.

Because I was so young, I assumed this trailer had the same
wooden area (more similar to a patio) as one of the other trailers

we lived in. I thought that she would just fall on those same wooden floors and not be hurt. I didn't realize that she would fall onto the ground. My cousins always did that to me, and I was okay every time; another lesson about observational learning.

Ironically, some of the earliest memories are of
someone letting me down
and me pushing someone away.

That would sum up my early years.

Fast forward a bit, and I started elementary school. I was so excited. I was tired of being stuck at home all day while my older sister got to go to school. I was also excited that I would finally be praised for doing well too. I wanted to be commended for being smart like my sister. I would study as long as I needed to. I would do whatever it took to have good grades.

My entire life... all I sought was acceptance and praise from my family. Now that I was in school, I was convinced that I would finally be able to get it. I thought that acceptance was something I had to earn. I was astonished when other kids would be praised by their parents for just *trying*. I thought that... to be loved... I needed to earn it.

I, of course, did not get it.

When I finally approached my parents, I demanded to know why they never bragged about me being smart. I asked why they never talked about how proud they were of my schooling. They did it for my sister, and I didn't understand why they seemed so ashamed of me. They never wanted to talk about me, while they would gush about others in my family. They would even praise my cousin for her grades in school. But not me.

They didn't seem to care about how it affected me. They would only mention it when I egged them on about it. They only did it to get me to stop talking about it and making them look bad.

I was very crushed by their response. I was told that my curriculum was just easier. Their excuse was that my grades "weren't the same grades." This meant that my A in kindergarten was the same as, if not worse than, the B my sister got in kindergarten. Or the C. Or any other grade.

I didn't know at the time that outside factors were causing what I saw as unfair treatment. During this time, my mother was so blinded by temporary gratification that she would end up destroying most of the familial relationships around her. This put a considerable strain on my parent's relationship. She had a few affairs during this time... leading to doubt on who my "real father" was.

My Nana revealed (and even my mother confessed) this to me years later... but at the time... I didn't know about the accusations of cheating. I wasn't aware that people were questioning who my "real father" was. Especially after a few people stepped forward to claim me as their own.

Whether it was true or not didn't matter...
the result was the same.
It had an impact on how they viewed me.
And that changed everything.

I didn't realize that I was being treated this way because I was a source of shame for my mother and a reminder of a deep hurt to my dad. Without knowing the real reason for this treatment, I had to come up with my own explanation. Around the age of seven or eight, when things went from neglect and occasional verbal abuse to physical abuse, I came up with my own reason. I rationalized it, you know... as best as a seven or eight-year-old could... and blamed it on myself.

If I were smarter, they would love me. If I were prettier, they would love me. If I listened more, they would love me. It's so devastating to me now that I could have possibly thought it was my fault my parents didn't love me. This faulty rationalization of a hopeless child just looking for answers led to an even worse one when I got older.

When I was on the verge of being a teenager, I started wondering if there was just something wrong with *me*. I wondered if something about me made it impossible for other people to love me. With a lack of love and affection from my parents and a revolving door of people coming in and out of my life, this is what I thought could explain it all. And all I wanted… more than anything else… was an explanation. I desperately desired an answer to all of my "why's."

To put it plain and simple, from then on, I thought I was unlovable. I thought there was no way that anyone could love me. I was born with a mark that only other people could see. My theory was that there had to be something wrong with me that was driving everyone away. I bought into this lie and explained away all the abusive behavior directed at me.

It was *my fault*.
I was just unlovable.

As a child (and even most times as an adolescent), you can't recognize the deeper issues at play. In my life, for example, I couldn't recognize that I was being treated differently because, to others, I was a reminder of infidelity. This inability to grasp such topics can lead to faulty rationalizations such as, "I am unlovable."

These rationalizations are called **schemas** — how we interpret and organize information. In basic terms, a schema is like a filing cabinet for our brain. There is a specific type of schema called "self-schema." These schemas can impact how we view ourselves and our relationship with others and the world around us.

The downside of self-schemas is that they can create faulty links. If I see that any relationship that I have been in (whether familial, romantic, platonic) has ended, been abusive, or completely one-sided… it can morph my schema, the framework that I use to understand what is going on around me, into thinking that I am unlovable.

This is precisely what I was doing. I was trying to rationalize something that I wasn't equipped to understand. I was trying to rationalize something I never should have been introduced to at that age. This damaging link between how my family treated me and my perception of myself was only solidified as I grew older. The idea that I was unlovable was becoming ingrained in me.

It formed my perception of myself.

If we're being honest... I liked this excuse because I didn't have to face the reality of my situation. If it was all because of *me*, my parents *could* love me after I fixed whatever was wrong with me.

If I could just figure out what that was, my parents would automatically start treating me like everyone else. I would no longer be the outcast. I would finally be loved. My life would become perfect after I could just figure out what it was about me that sent people running in the opposite direction.

This lie made it hard for me to understand or accept the idea of God's love. The people who were supposed to love me unconditionally did not. I refused to accept that God's love could be so great. Every other love I had experienced had failed me and deeply hurt me.

Every other "love" left me feeling
paralyzed, exploited, powerless, and *insignificant*.
As a result, I felt I couldn't trust any kind of love.
I didn't want to be hurt again.

I bought into this lie for most of my life. But the thing is...God always shows up and illustrates His love for me. He will show me in the quiet when I'm full of doubt. He'll show me in the storm when everything seems to be overpowering me. He'll show me during the days when all is going well... when I don't feel like I need Him.

Sometimes it's a reminder in the little things. A bright penny laying in front of me when I'm stressed about finances... a reminder that He really does provide. Other times it's a picture of a lighthouse when I'm worried about which path I should take... a reminder that His light will guide my path.

But it's also in the big things. He shows me that it's okay that I can't fully understand His love because it is incomprehensible (Ephesians 3:19). Why would perfection die for those flawed all the way down to their innermost being? The extraordinary power of His love stretches far beyond our understanding. He shows me that I can trust in His love -- even when I cannot trust in anyone else's -- because His love is not like any other love.

It is so much greater.
His love leaves me feeling *cared for*, *held*, *safe*, and *valued*.

*"And to know the love of Christ, **which passeth knowledge**, that ye might be filled with*
all the fulness of God."
Ephesians 3:19 (KJV)

Sometimes God uses people to show me His love...and shows me that His love is *still* much more than the love they have for me. It blows my mind every time.

Harrison is definitely one of those people. He helped me understand God's love through his actions. Harrison also helped me accept the love of God when I couldn't understand it. He showed me a glimpse of what God's love is like.

Growing up, my example of love was constant shouting and verbalizing threats. Sometimes those threats were acted on. Quite frankly, *most times*, those threats were acted on. In public. In private. In church. At home. It didn't matter where we were. We were the family you saw in Walmart having a knock-down-drag-out fight in the middle of the meat section.

My example of love was constantly demeaning the other person and acting out of a complete lack of trust. Demanding all the passwords of the other. Continually monitoring all text messages… even from family members. Projecting their cheating onto the other. Calling each other names in public with no care about who hears. Telling embarrassing secrets about the other without thinking about how it would make the other feel.

My example of love was turning to others outside of the marriage when times got tough. Not caring how those actions affected the other. Not being willing to work on simple communication problems. Never being willing to admit when they were wrong. Constantly wanting to put all blame on the other party (something that I have noticed really shaped my style of arguing).

Wanting to throw in the towel when there was still plenty of hope just for the sake of laziness.

I didn't want anything to do with that, hence the plan to resort to *a loveless* marriage to escape if needed. If that was what love was, then I didn't want it. In a loveless marriage, I wouldn't care about cheating. I would only stay married long enough to escape my home. We would get divorced later, and then I would be able to really live my life. I viewed marriage as just a means to an end.

When I started dating Harrison, I was astonished by how healthily he approached things. Harrison was the opposite of my parents. He wanted to solve problems before they became a more significant issue. He wanted to have open and honest communication. Harrison never wanted to throw in the towel. Ever. Even when I fully expected him to.

He showed me that not all love is distorted, manipulative, or disingenuous.

While dating Harrison, I learned how to love people and *express* it to them -- something I've always struggled with out of fear of rejection. He basically taught me how to be social and all the proper etiquette I was never taught by my parents. That sounds really sad, doesn't it? A sixteen-year-old learning everything that a parent should have taught her from her high school boyfriend?

His family would do the same. I was given an understanding of what family was really like — what it meant to truly love another person. From them… I learned what it was like to give love that was reciprocated. To love beyond condition. I was amazed by their family dynamic. It was like a complete cultural shock.

Acceptance.

Encouragement.
So much support.
I couldn't believe that this was what family could be.

This comfort with love made me able to accept friendships. Real friendships, not surface-level friendliness. I made friends who supported me in everything I set my mind to. Ones who didn't only speak to me when they needed something. Friends that genuinely wanted to see me happy. Ones who would lovingly call me out when I was doing something wrong. Gently correcting me where I needed it.

For the first time in my life,
I knew what healthy love looked like.
A romantic love.
A familial love.
And a platonic love.

Now… when I look at the ring on my finger that I thought would never actually mean something to me… I'm not just reminded of the love Harrison has for me; I'm also reminded of the love God has for me.

A love that supersedes all other loves. One that is unchanging. Constant. One that will never fade. One that I don't have to worry will disappear when I wake up in the morning or go to sleep at night. His love is perfect and casts out all those fears (1 John 4:18).

A love that is so great we can never wholly fathom it (Ephesians 3:19).

Remember, you aren't unlovable. You're not at fault. There are people who will love you. There are people who will care for you. It is possible to find them -- I am a witness. I have experienced it. Love Himself has proven that you can be loved.

Saying you're unlovable is like saying that God isn't merciful or gracious enough to love you despite all you've done.

According to the Miriam-Webster dictionary, unlovable means to be "incapable of inspiring love or admiration." This means that it is *impossible* for others to love you. Looking at the definition alone… it is *factually* incorrect.

We aren't unlovable because He loves us.
The verbiage we use is important.

Even if the rest of the world despises you, *He* does not. He loves us. You will always have Him. It's essential to watch the wording we use — saying we are unlovable is false. He can love us.

*"The Lord is not slack concerning his promise, as some men count slackness; but is longsuffering to us-ward, **not willing that any should perish, but that all should come to repentance.**" 2 Peter 3:9 (KJV)*

God wants us all to come to repentance. He wants us all to be saved. That's how much He loves you. More than you'll ever know. His love supersedes all other loves, so don't let the other loves (or lack thereof) define you.

CHAPTER FOUR:
Trust the God of the Process

*"And they overcame him by the blood of the Lamb, **and by the word of their testimony;*** *and they loved not their lives unto the death."*
— *Revelation 12:11 (KJV)*

I've always struggled with expressing my thoughts and emotions, which is why I was so scared when I felt God leading me to write this book. The idea of strangers learning things about me that took me years to express to someone I loved and trusted terrified me... petrified me.. paralyzed me.

As a result of this struggle, I had to work through many expressions and emotions that I had repressed. It also meant writing about things that weren't known by many people. The perfect image my family tried to create fooled many people. There would be some that would be hearing about this for the first time. That scared me. I almost let it silence me.

For so many years, I was silenced.
Out of insecurity.
Out of fear.
Sometimes by force.

So often, I was told what I had to say didn't matter and that I should just "keep my mouth shut." So I did. And I was silenced for so long that I would sometimes forget that I did... in fact... have a voice. I *did* have something to say.

In elementary school, I was the weird girl who never spoke. Ever. This is what many people knew me as -- the odd quiet girl. I didn't talk much... not during lunch, not during recess, and especially not during class; teachers would ask me questions, and I wouldn't respond. It was so bad that quite a few times, people assumed I was mute.

I learned years later that this is actually something that happens to children who experience abuse. It's called selective mutism. In a basic sense of the meaning, it is when children are unable to speak in certain situations despite being able to communicate in other situations. It's a childhood disorder, so it goes away (in most cases) with time. I didn't understand this then.

I thought that…
once again…
There was something deeply wrong with <i>me</i>.

It got so bad that I was hauled into the office of the school speech therapist. The teachers speculated that I had a speech impediment that made me too self-conscious to speak. Some thought that I was just trying to get out of work. Whatever the reasoning, they acknowledged that my behavior was not "normal."

I walked into the speech therapist's office and was almost immediately sent back out. It became very evident I was *choosing* to be silent. This left some teachers scratching their heads, while it raised a few suspicions with some of the other faculty at school. These suspicions were quickly dismissed.

What no one else knew was that I was silenced by insecurity. An insecurity caused by the negative voices that echoed in my head. No one cared about what I had to say, so why bother trying? Everyone was going to laugh at me. Why bring humiliation upon myself? So anytime I was in a situation where there was a power imbalance… anytime I felt inferior to someone… I couldn't speak. It wasn't that I didn't *want* to… it felt like I couldn't.

In the first of many elementary schools I attended, you filed into the lunch line in the classroom, and that was the order you sat in. This meant that I often had people from another class sitting in front of me.

I had no friends at this particular elementary school. In fact, I attended multiple elementary schools because I was constantly moving around Northeast Arkansas... so I never really had friends.

Since I didn't have friends, I filed in the lunch line randomly and had no one to talk to every time. Quite a few times, another kid would ask me to switch spots with them because they wanted to sit by the other kid in front of me. But I was always alone.

This resulted in me eavesdropping on whichever kids were sitting across from me. I didn't want them to know that I was listening to what they were saying, so I would act distracted by things like the back of a milk carton or my tray. I felt so alone, but I still never spoke a word. No one wanted to talk to me. I felt ostracized... everyone else seemed to get along so well.

No one else seemed to be struggling the way I was.
What was wrong with me?

In high school, I was a little better at not being scared to talk to people and express myself... but I was still struggling with it. I was quiet and only spoke to a few people I felt comfortable around.

My learned shyness was so bad that my geometry teacher gave me the "mime award" on the small awards day she held in her class at the end of the year. My teachers seemed to like calling me out for it, and I very much needed it. As I said, I was convinced that what I had to say didn't matter and I was so used to being silenced that I just didn't speak unless directly spoken to.

But there's more to the story. Along with the insecurity, the second underlying factor was that I was also terrified of accidentally giving a peek into the reality of my world. You see, I had mastered the act of putting on the mask of the normal, always-happy-Kimi in high school. By my junior year, one girl even asked me how I could always be so happy. She had no idea that I was actually crumbling behind the mask.

No one suspected that I was actually dying inside.

No one knew I was experiencing things I wouldn't be able to talk about for years when I walked out of that high school building. I fooled everyone, and that was *mostly due to* my silence.

I thought I wouldn't accidentally give anything away if I didn't talk much. I didn't want to pay the consequences of revealing the truth. The idea of accidentally making a joke or a side comment that revealed what was really going on worried me. No one could know the truth. This may seem like an overreaction, but I assure you it was not.

> Even with my silence,
> I let things slip…
> more than once.

As a kid, I thought what was happening to me was normal. I didn't have the cognitive ability at the time (or the exposure to the social norms of families to tell me what was happening to me was wrong) to understand that abuse wasn't okay. I tried to convince myself that they loved me; that was just how they showed it.

Because of this, I accidentally let it slip sometimes. One night, it all came to a head when I made a slip at church. I don't remember exactly what I said, but it was enough to make people question how we were treated when no one was around. What resulted was hours of screaming. "Why don't you just stop speaking?" "You ruin everything every time you open up that big mouth of yours." "No one cares about what you have to say anyway." Those are just a few quotes I remember.

This is what spurred my silence. I internalized those words. This sparked years of speaking only when spoken to — outside of my few friends. It extended well beyond that, and sometimes I catch myself staying quiet to this day out of habit. Even when I have something to say.

> But it didn't just happen in elementary.
> I had a slip in high school as well.

On picture day of my junior year, my (now) husband's best friend stole my phone and hid it in his shirt pocket. This had been something we were doing to each other all week, so it wasn't out of malice. It became a joke among our group.

The problem came when he didn't reveal that he had stolen it. Typically, we would reveal within a couple of minutes that we stole the other person's phone. Then everyone would proceed to laugh, and we would carry on as usual.

Instead, this time he had gotten too distracted taking pictures and went to class... forgetting that my phone was in his pocket. After I took my picture, I walked back to class with Harrison. We were joking around. Laughing. We tried to take as long as we could because we didn't want to sit around in class. At this point, I still didn't realize I didn't have my phone.

When we returned to the band room, I *still* didn't notice it was missing. Since it was picture day, we weren't rehearsing as a group because there would be too many interruptions. After sitting down for a couple of minutes, I finally realized that I had left my phone in the cafeteria (or so I thought), and Harrison walked with me to look for it.

There I realized that the phone was not on the table where I (thought) I had left it... cue the alarm bells. I looked everywhere. I searched the table, under the table, and the stage. I even went as far as digging through the trash. That's right... I searched through mounds of milk cartons, eggs, and soggy cereal to find that phone.

With no luck in my search, I slowly made my way back to the band room. At this point, the panic was setting in. I was crying, shaking, and having difficulty catching my breath. I was in mid-panic attack and sitting in the band room.... crying uncontrollably in front of everyone.

To the outsider, it looked like I was overreacting about my phone. In reality, I was freaking out about the consequences I would face for losing my phone. My sister once broke her phone getting off the bus, and the blame was still somehow placed on me. I didn't want to know the consequences of *me* actually *losing* a phone.

I was clearly not in a stable state of being.
This is where the big slip happened.

I was surrounded by Harrison (who at this point knew a little about what was really going on in my life, but not a lot), my best friend, and two other girls. I'm not going to use the real names of these girls for privacy reasons, so for the purpose of this story, I am calling them K and S.

These girls were people I was comfortable with. I wouldn't say that we were close friends, but I felt comfortable around them. We were in the process of trying to use Find My iPhone on Harrison's phone to track mine down.

I couldn't remember my password, but it did have an option to change my password since I was having trouble logging in. S suggested I use a password like Fingernail13 — something random but also crazy, so there was no way I would forget again. It was an excellent tip, and I was grateful for her help later on.

Everyone around me was trying to assure me that I was okay. They kept telling me that it was just a phone and it would be found. Or even if I never found the phone... it was just a phone. A few people tried to reassure me by saying that it wasn't a big deal and it would eventually pop up — that there was no reason to cry.

"You can always get a new one."

This just made me feel worse. There was no way my parents would get me a new one. And they most certainly wouldn't think, "it's not a big deal." They would have a lot to say and do about it. And I would be sore the next day.

No one understood the real reason I was so panicked. And my mid-panic attack brain started feeling stupid... so it got defensive. It decided to explain a little of why I was so worked up. I started repeatedly saying, "I'm going to be punched in the face... they're going to kill me." Everyone around me once again jumped to calm me.

Everyone assured me I would not be in that much trouble... except S. She looked at me very puzzled and said, "You're going to be punched in the face?" I don't know if she caught on at that moment and realized what was really going on; I might have read too much into it... but I felt like she knew. And to this day, I still mostly feel like she realized what my life was really like in that short moment.

Long story short, the best friend came to the band room with my phone after a few calls finally went through. He felt horrible, and I felt so guilty for making him feel that way. I wasn't mad at him at all, but everyone else was. I was overwhelmed with relief that he did have my phone. Everyone was giving him such a hard time. I was always viewed by most people around me as someone needing protection because of how small I was... little did they know I really needed it.

I just didn't need it in the way they were giving it. The whole ordeal made me feel so guilty. I didn't want Harrison's best friend to feel like he made me cry... because he didn't make me cry.

It took a couple of hours for me to fully calm down as I had gone through *every single possible* scenario had I not found my phone the entire time it was missing. Once my head was clear, I realized what I had done.

Now people knew.
Even if they didn't connect it right now, they knew.
Those two phrases explained all of my behavior and why I
was always so anxious... so on edge.

But those two phrases also cracked the shell that I had around my story. They were minimal... probably cracks that no one would notice... but they were there. Before this experience, I was on a fruitless mission to deny my own reality because it was too messy for me to accept. After this experience, I was opened up to the long road of processing my trauma instead of masking it under a denial of its existence.

I had finally admitted to what I
was experiencing out loud.
That changed everything.
There can be so much power in the spoken word.

And that's the reality of trauma. We can spend so long trying to deny its existence. It hinders us mentally, spiritually, and even physically (if you're interested, do some research on somatic symptoms brought on by stress, anxiety, PTSD, etc., – it's such an intriguing topic). Denying the existence of pain doesn't make it hurt any less.

If you're still shackled by the pain a divorce (yours, your parents, etc.) caused you... that's trauma. If you are still overwhelmed by what happened in your childhood... that's trauma. If you're still impacted by an addiction (yours, your parents, etc.) — that's trauma. If something you've experienced still affects your daily living... *that's trauma.* If you're still carrying it with you, it needs to be addressed. If it is something that has changed the way that you look at or view yourself, the people around you, or the world (environment) around you... it's trauma. It must be treated.

Many studies have shown that untreated trauma can result in a continuation of the cycle of abuse, addiction, strained relationships, and/or deteriorated social well-being. If you have the time, I recommend reading peer-reviewed articles on this topic if you want a deeper understanding of this.

> The bottom line is that we can't live
> our lives behind a mask.
> We have to acknowledge our pain.
> We have to be honest about our emotions.
>
> You can't heal from something when you
> act like it isn't there.
> Don't sweep it under the rug.

There are many ways to go about treating trauma. I go into this a lot more in-depth in chapter seven. I highly suggest you find a method that works best for your individual process. And always remember that it is okay to seek out professional help.

Sometimes trauma can be worked through in a couple of weeks. Sometimes it may take many years to work through. Sometimes it takes a lifetime. And sometimes, it can happen in an instant. The road to recovery is unique to each individual experience. My road doesn't look like exactly yours, and yours doesn't look exactly like mine... and that's okay.

Whatever you do, make sure to keep God at the center. He is the ultimate physician. I've never known a peace sweeter than the one He gives. I've never known a love more remarkable than the one He wraps me in.

When you are processing your trauma... whether through therapy, talking to a friend, or just working through it on your own first... make sure that you speak to Him about it. Don't feel like you must be all put together to approach God.

We can't fool Him;
we don't need to try.

Writing has always been my coping mechanism. When I was younger, I would create my own worlds while I walked to school. It would distract me from the pain I was experiencing in the real world. This book started from a journal and became what it is now. Writing has always been a healthy way for me to cope.

I can vent out my frustrations without the worry of someone else seeing it. I can work through what I am facing and devise a plan to tackle it. I can recognize the lessons I am learning during that season and have them to fall back on when I'm facing a similar one in the future.

While you're in the process of recovery... of any kind of recovery... try to find healthy ways to cope. Exercise is a great one (in moderation). Listening to music or playing an instrument is as well. Find one that works best for you. But one I suggest... even if you don't think of yourself as a writer... is writing down prayers. Write down the things you're scared to say out loud. Go to Him with your worries.

Almost always, the process... you're going to be blown away by this one... will be a process. More than likely, it won't be instant. You won't wake up suddenly feeling different. You won't magically feel whole.

Nearly every time... it takes *time*.

After experiencing many years of abuse — emotional, physical, and more — I began to develop physical and emotional scars.

Those deep, invisible scars really affected me. It impacted my behavior. It impacted how I thought about myself and others. It touched every aspect of my life.

I started to think: "How do you move past something that tormented your soul for so many years?" "How do you heal from something that took eighteen years to develop?"

I found that the answer was simple: WE don't do anything about it. Work on ourselves? Sure. Take steps to come to a deeper understanding? Definitely. But we don't have the power to transform *our hearts*. We do not hold the ability to *heal* ourselves. Healing comes from the One with the only saving name.

I'm reminded of the woman with the issue of blood (Luke 8:43-48). For twelve years, she was tormented by bleeding that was out of her control. It impacted every area of her life, more than we realize on a surface-level read-through. Countless doctors tried to fix it; she went as far as spending "all of her living on physicians" (Luke 8:43). She probably tried many at-home remedies to stop the problem as well.

She realized that her issue was something that was out of her control. It was too much for her to handle on her own. She couldn't heal herself. She realized that if she only touched the smallest portion of Christ, she would be healed. She knew that He was able... and Jesus responded with,

"Daughter, be of good comfort:
thy faith hath saved thee; go in peace."
— Luke 8:48 (KJV)

I couldn't do anything to heal the scars. They ran too deep for me to fix on my own. It was too much for me to handle. Like the woman with the issue of blood, I recognized that I could not heal myself.

For years, I never thought I would be able to be where I am now. The scars aren't entirely gone, and there have been a few new ones in the past few years. But I am in such a healthier mental state than I was then. A healthier mental state than I have ever been in before.

We can't heal ourselves, but we have faith in
Someone who can.
He can do what we can't even begin to attempt.

During that time of waiting…
During the time of uncertainty…
During the time when it seems you'll never know "why"…
Trust the God of the process…
The only One who can save.

CHAPTER FIVE:
The Dawn of Restoration

"Again, a new commandment I write unto you,
which thing is true in him and in you:
because the darkness is past,
and the true light now shineth."
— 1 John 2:8 (KJV)

I moved around a lot as a kid. As I've mentioned, I moved every single year until I was in the 6th grade. I rarely had time to make real friends. Not only was I facing all the horrible things at my home, but I was facing them alone; I often didn't have a friend to confide in. During this stage of my life – around the age of nine to eleven – I developed confidence issues.

I was doing great on the academic side of school... but I was failing on the social side. Making friends was not an easy task for me. I didn't have much experience socializing, so I didn't know what to say or do to make people like me. I always felt like an outsider... like I wasn't normal. It made it hard for me to relate to other kids.

Because of this – and my lack of healthy interaction with my parents – my social skills were stunted. I grew to be resentful of my parents because of this. This lack of experience greatly impacted all of my later relationships. This was where the bitterness toward my parents really began.

I was very awkward and *still* can be. I didn't know how to start conversations and could never figure out how to keep the conversation going. You can't make friends when you don't know how to talk to people. And you can't keep friends when you revert into yourself and/or run away after every awkward interaction.

So I was alone…
as always.

I would sit on the monkey bars by myself. I was surrounded by other kids, but they were all playing with each other. My favorite spot on the playground was the merry-go-round. I could stand there while it was spinning, and it wasn't so apparent that I didn't have friends.

It was where I first noticed Harrison, so it was good for me in the long run. He was great at spinning the merry-go-round fast. I thought he was cool because of it. And because he wore sandals... none of the other boys were wearing sandals. But nonetheless, I was also alone at home. Most days during this time, I hid (or was locked up) in my room.

Being stuck by yourself in isolation gives you plenty of time to think, as we all learned in 2020 due to the pandemic. I would spend the majority of my days in elementary and junior high school alone. I thought a lot about my situation with all that time alone. I was struggling socially, and I needed an answer for why.

I decided that I was the problem... again.
You might start to notice a pattern here.

That's all I was hearing. I was always at fault, so why would this be any different? It was then that I started trying on different personalities. I tried to morph into whatever I thought would get people to like me. I would try on a mask and quickly move on to the next if it didn't get the response I was expecting.

I felt like no one was there for me.
I felt like no one wanted me.
I felt unlovable at first,
but at this time in my life...
I felt abandoned as well.

I wasn't receiving much support at home. I always felt overshadowed by my sisters — nothing I did was as good as them. One of them was always viewed as the adorable one. The other was the smart one. The other two being the "best behaved." I was always told I was the shy or quiet one, and I never really viewed that as a compliment. In their eyes, I didn't deserve attention because I wasn't as good as my other siblings. And I never really got it. You can imagine what that does to a kid.

As time passed by, it seemed like
my life went further down a never-ending spiral
toward depression, abuse, severe loneliness, and anxiety.

As I grew, my home life got worse and worse. Somewhere along the way, my parents started drifting from the church. They started out just making "small" compromises. These compromises lead them to skip a few services. "It's only Wednesday night... nothing important will happen." During this time, I didn't have anyone to pick me up. So if they didn't go, then I didn't go. Before long, we stopped going to church entirely.

Next came alcohol in the fridge. I remember almost drinking a hard lemonade when I was maybe eight or nine. It traumatized me a little because my mother reacted so viscerally. I thought it was just lemonade, but it was my parents' disguise, so they didn't have to feel guilty for getting drunk.

It looked like lemonade.
It smelled like lemonade.
It tasted like lemonade.
So in their eyes, it wasn't *real* alcohol.

Small compromises that didn't seem like a big deal at the time ultimately led to things they probably never imagined they would do. That's always how it starts. A little compromise here and another one there. Eventually, it leads to a lifestyle you once thought was impossible for you to slip into. The compromises of my parents led to them no longer striving to live a life pursuing godliness... something they once said they would never do.

The further my parents drifted from their few years of being in church, the worse the abuse got. When I was younger, I was beaten with a belt, a paddle (that had my older sister and I's names written on it), a branch with thorns (my mom once bragged about this one when talking about "discipline"), a fly swat, a spoon, a shoe, etc. If you can name it, I have probably been hit with it.

Now, I understand that children should be disciplined. Still, there is a very defined line between discipline and abuse that my father very frequently crossed. He didn't care about the line as long as he got his point across. It didn't matter how many bruises it left or how many tears it caused. Many other family members could be the same way when they wanted to be.

Discipline is good for a child, but *abuse* is not. If your "discipline" causes your child to be forced to wear a long sleeve shirt the next day to hide bruises, it is no longer discipline.

Suppose you're like me, and you grew up in a home that wasn't touchy-feely at all (unless you were getting "disciplined"). In that case, you may understand why it was once (and sometimes still is) hard for me to express my emotions. My example of love was dysfunctional love. I couldn't tell anyone "I love you" until Harrison because I didn't even know what love was.

Real, healthy love was a foreign concept to me for so long. We didn't sit around the table for a family dinner. I was never read bedtime stories, I wasn't tucked in at night, and no one ever checked for monsters under my bed or in the closet. Sadly, in my case, the monsters I feared were the ones sleeping in the bed just a few doors over.

I experienced constant belittling. Sometimes they would build me up a little with the sole purpose of tearing me back down. Leading me to the rug and then pulling it right out from underneath me. To me, the scars left on me from physical abuse could not compare to the ones left inside me from emotional and verbal abuse.

I didn't really know what it was like to be loved until I was a teenager. I sometimes saw my dad take out all of his anger on my mother during my early years. I even walked in on him choking her once. As I got older, the abuse shifted from focusing on my mother to being directed solely on me.

I think that's at the core of why I couldn't tell anyone. I was afraid that if I told someone about the abuse and got out of the situation, the focus would shift back to her — better me than anyone else. What happened to me didn't matter, and she would never have to deal with it again. That was an attitude I was trained to always have. Constantly feeling the pressure to take care of everyone, but never making time to care for me. To ensure everyone else was safe and happy, even to my detriment.

That made me feel like the pain had a a purpose.

Eventually, my mother decided to listen to my pleas and move back to Lake City. That was where my best friend from my kindergarten, "H", was.

She was one of the few kids who approached me and wouldn't let me ignore her. The first time I met H, she walked up to me and wouldn't stop talking. I liked listening more than talking, so we were a good pair. Lake City was where she lived; moving back meant I could see her again.

Lake City was where I was the happiest. It always has been. This move happened when I was in the fourth grade, so it was at the start of the boy craze. One of my mother's friends learned that we moved back and offered to take us to church the weekend we moved (the weekend before school). We went, it seemed fun, and I liked it a lot.

Plus, I saw a boy that I thought was really cute, but my glasses were broken, so I couldn't *really* see him. This boy turned out to be Harrison, and his dad was the church's new pastor. The funny thing about this situation is that this was also Harrison's first year at Riverside. And with us being the same age, we were about to be in school together.

He remembers seeing me for the first time ever at school, but all I remember is his mother saying, "didn't we see you at church last night?" when she noticed me as she walked through the door. She was a grownup talking *directly* to me, so I panicked and ran to some friends I remembered from when I used to go to school there. Harrison says he remembers standing with some friends from his street who were goofing off by the couch at the back of the room. And by what would seem like fate found only in a fairytale, not only were those friends of his the same friends of mine from before... but out of the two homeroom options for fourth grade (it was a small school), we shared the same one. As I walked up and joined the group, he turned around and was "stunned" to see "the most beautiful girl ever" standing in front of him. He even remembers my exact outfit down to the glasses I wore. It's an adorable story.

But before all of that. Before Harrison's mother terrified me. Before Harrison saw me for the first time...I walked into the doors of the school I attended in Kindergarten. I was so happy but quickly realized I didn't remember anyone besides H and a few others. I thought I remembered hanging out with a girl we'll call "C" (who was also friends with H), but I couldn't remember what she looked like.

The principal took my hand and led me to the cafeteria. She introduced me to a girl, "A," that would show me around. We quickly became best friends. Soon, I would spend almost every weekend at her house. Since we stayed inside the whole time, I didn't find out until later that she not only lived on the same street as Harrison... but they were even next-door neighbors. The first weekend I went to her house, I was ecstatic. A weekend full of no fears, no worrying about where my next meal would come from, no creepy guys being invited over, and NO pain. I was finally going to get a break.

I was living the life.

When we woke that Sunday morning, she asked me if I wanted to go to church with her. She explained the church and said it was called the Pentecostals of Lake City. Instantly, I linked this church with a church I used to attend. I liked that church, so surely I would like this one, right?

She and the rest of the kids on the street would catch a ride from her neighbor. I followed her as she ran out of the door to their driveway. To my surprise, it was *the same church* my mom's friend had taken me to, and Harrison's mother was the neighbor picking us up. While at church, I met many boys from school I didn't see that week.

I didn't meet any new girls my age (it was just me and A), but that didn't deter me from going. Life was so exciting during this stage. I loved learning more and more about God. I felt completely safe when I entered the church building… something I wasn't used to feeling.

Nothing could possibly go wrong here.

My friend seemed to really enjoy this church as well. We would go almost every Sunday for years... until one day, she stopped wanting to wake up so early on a Sunday. It was one of her days off from school, and she wanted to sleep in.

Being the shy person I was, I didn't go when Harrison walked up to the door to let us know they were leaving. I watched the van drive away from the window. And for the first time... I wasn't in it.

I didn't get to learn a new lesson. I didn't get to volunteer to read. I missed snack time. No one asked me if I had memorized the memory verse. I felt so empty. More so than I usually did. I was honestly bummed for the rest of the day. Sunday morning was my only chance to feel free. I decided at that moment that I would go next time, even if my friend didn't.

So that next Sunday, I decided to pack up my bag and go anyway. It was then that we started drifting from each other. It wasn't her fault, but we kept becoming more and more different. I was devastated because she was my one and only *real* friend during this time of my life. Her house had become my escape.

I grew so attached to her. I went everywhere with her. I did everything with her. I didn't think I could survive school without her... and that terrified me. I started to panic. At some point, she would get tired of me as everyone else did. She was going to leave just as everyone else did. I was convinced she would. We were inseparable...until we became so starkly different.

I then decided I would fix the problem... or so I mistakenly thought at the time. I was going to stop being friends with her before she got tired of me. My parents were already telling me that she was showing the signs. They kept telling me that she didn't really like me and would soon ditch me for our mutual friend. They said that they heard her talking to others about her plan to get rid of me.

They would make up sources for information like this, but I would still believe them every time. They were highly trained in gaslighting me, so I easily believed everything they said. When I didn't initially believe them, they would make me feel like I was "crazy" for not believing them. They wouldn't stop talking about it until they realized they had successfully convinced me of it.

I heard this repeatedly for weeks. You can only hear something for so long before you start believing it; I started believing it. Then I did something foolish that I regret to this day. I saw her family as the perfect family, and I was jealous of her. I decided that the solution was to do something to get "back at her."

Starting a fight with the purpose of ending the friendship before she could... that wasn't wise. It made me feel horrible. But when I told my parents what happened, they told me that it was better than what she had planned to do.

I always tried to hurt others before they could hurt me. I did this a lot. When someone got too close, I pushed them away. She was getting too close, and I sabotaged the relationship before she could find out the truth. I could feel her drifting because of how different we were becoming, and I wanted to end the friendship before she did.

I was acting out what I saw at home.
I wanted to feel like I didn't
actually want to be her friend,
when I was really dying inside to keep the friendship alive.

We eventually stopped being friends. It was entirely my fault. She hung out with a different set of girls than I did. We didn't hate each other, but an awkwardness between us lingered on afterward. At this point, A didn't go to our church often, but she still came from time to time.

This new relationship between us freaked me out, and it was my fault. I still wanted to go to church, but she went there first. If anyone was supposed to stop going, it was me. I thought about it and concluded that since she didn't go much anymore, there was no real reason for me to stop going. We didn't hate each other, so if I did go... it wouldn't be *too* awkward. I listened to myself this time.

Over a decade later,

I'm so glad that I did.

I kept going. My friend eventually stopped coming for good; she started attending a different church. Most of the kids our age did the same. Some of them moved away. Some of them switched churches. And a few of them quit going altogether. It quickly became only Harrison, Clayton (my friend and Harrison's cousin), and I in our age group.
After a couple of months (maybe even a year) of me attending the church, I convinced my sisters to go with me *all the time*. So even though there were only 3 people my age, I could still depend on my sisters to keep me company. And there I was... the only "bus kid" (besides my sisters) left.
Eventually, my older sister got married and moved away. My younger sister would hang out with the younger kids who started coming, leaving me all alone during times of fellowship. I was in a youth group with three boys, and I couldn't keep up with the talk of sports, hunting, and fishing. At the time, at least... I am pretty good at fishing and Fantasy Football now though. I still don't hunt yet.
I still enjoyed going to church, but I always felt alone. No matter how many attempts the church made to make me feel like I belonged, I always felt like I didn't. Regardless of the many attempts to fix how I felt, I couldn't help but feel alone.
This ruined my mood. I felt unloved at home and at school. I never felt unloved at church, but as I said, being in a youth group of only boys could really make you feel left out sometimes.

I felt like I didn't belong anywhere.

The boys would even try to hold conversations I could follow, but it never worked out. We had nothing in common, and I was way too shy at that point in my life. I couldn't relate to their problems, and I couldn't offer solutions. I didn't understand what life was like as a teenage boy.
I got really discouraged during those few years. My friend "M" would come with me every now and then. It was a significant improvement from my interaction with the boys because I finally

had someone to talk to when the topic went to something I didn't know much about.

But M lived in Paragould (where I used to live), so coming to Lake City wasn't something that could happen often. That meant she would go with me about twice a month.

When she didn't, I felt alone. I had friends at school, but I would only consider two close and reliable. The boys were friendly with me at church, so I would consider them friends at church. But I had no one outside of school and church. This feeling of being alone became unbearable. Everywhere I went, I felt like I didn't belong. I felt like an imposter.

I wasn't reading or praying daily at this point in my life. I read my Bible all the way through once for the first time in sixth grade...and I didn't really pick it back up consistently afterward.

Around this time, I knew something needed to change. I knew I shouldn't feel like this... that God didn't want me to feel this way. I was alone and sad. Nothing helped. Not hours of binge-watching tv shows. Not hanging out with my few friends. Even crying didn't give me relief.

Usually, I could cry and feel better after. There came the point where that didn't even work anymore.

I cried so much that I couldn't cry anymore.

If I were to summarize my story
(especially during this time),
I would use 1 John 2:8:

*"Again, a new commandment I write unto you, which thing is true in him and in you: **because the darkness is past, and the true light now shineth.** "(KJV)*

For years of my life, I was engulfed in darkness. It surrounded me spiritually, physically, and mentally. I was lost. I was hopeless. I was constantly living in a state of "why me?"

In the spirit of transparency, I didn't want to be alive at this point in my life. I didn't see the point of living. I was experiencing so many damaging things at one time, and I couldn't see any hope.

I didn't think I would ever get out of my situation, so I didn't see the point of living anymore. What's the point of continuing on?

When I was in junior high (up until the start of high school), I was suicidal. No one knew. I'm going to be brutally honest here because frequently, when we read a book, we view the author as perfect.

They *have* to be... they've written a book! But when writing a book, authors sometimes write out all the negatives. They aren't transparent due to fear of the opinion of others. The truth may change how others view them.

I'm getting to the point in my process where I am no longer allowing my story to continue to be locked inside due to the fear of unknown opinions. The people who are going to talk can find anything to talk about. They will *always* find something to talk about. I'm now okay with the talk being about my story. Maybe someone will overhear it and find hope that God can deliver them too.

Here is me showing more transparency than I have ever been able to in my entire life: I had a plan for my life, and it could go two ways. I either had to get married as soon as possible, or I had to die.

I'm not going to sugarcoat this time of my life as I had in earlier editions of this chapter because I feel it's crucial for you to know how dark this time really was for me. I was miserable. I was being abused. I felt alone in my darkness.

It all came to a head after one particularly horrible night. After hours of being berated and receiving many threats, I ran to my room.

Hopeless... again.
Confused... again.
Angry... again.

So many emotions were swirling around in my head...
threatening to spill out.

I could still hear their voices ringing in my ears. Years of physical abuse, constant degrading, and being told that their lives would be easier if I wasn't here hit a boiling point. At this point, I wasn't just contemplating suicide, as I had many times before... I was going to go through with it.

For real this time.

It seemed much sooner and more guaranteed than the marriage option. So that was the decision I was prepared to make. For months, I had a plan in case I ever felt brave enough to go through with it. At this moment, I thought that I was. I was so done with everything. I couldn't handle any more of what I was experiencing. I was tired of crying every day. I was tired of feeling worthless. I was tired of trying to survive. It was so much effort to keep going. I didn't feel like I was strong enough anymore.

How do you keep going and living life when the worst things keep happening to you? How do you keep making it through the day when you know the next one might be ten times worse? How do you keep fighting to stay alive when everything seems to lead you to this plan?

The answer was Jesus and will always be Jesus.

By the grace of God, I decided to pull out my Bible one last time. I had no intention of changing my plan, but I wanted to be calm when I went through with it. I was overwhelmed by emotion from the abuse I was enduring, and I knew that any time I read the Bible, I felt peace. Once again... by the grace of God... I started reading in the New Testament (I think it was Matthew — but definitely one of the Gospels). I started crying. Full-on ugly crying. I could not comprehend how someone could love me so much that they would die for me. And such a brutal death at that. The idea of someone caring for me that much just shook me to my core. I decided (like the old cliche saying goes) that if He could die for me, I could continue living for Him. Literally.

When I opened that Bible, I felt the peace I expected. But I didn't expect it to change my life... in one moment. I couldn't help but cry as I read through those chapters. I could never imagine Someone loving me so much that they would give their life for me.

I didn't feel loved for the longest time, so this shocked me. I never knew that there was a love much greater than anyone in this world could ever give me.

This day sparked something in me that would change the trajectory of my life.

In the midst of tragedy, there still remains light.
When we look for it, we are guaranteed to see it.
Your testimony lies in that light.
Never stop in your journey towards that light.

CHAPTER SIX:
The Importance of Prayer

"Continue in prayer,
and watch in the same with thanksgiving."
— 1 John 2:8 (KJV)

The Bible makes it very clear in 2 Timothy 3:16 that every scripture in the Bible is inspired by God. When we read His Word, it satisfies our soul as nothing else can. It helps us grow in faith and gives us direction. It provides peace and joy that no worldly thing could ever offer.

When you distance yourself from God's Word, you make yourself more vulnerable to believing Satan's lies, which drain the peace and joy out of your life. The lies nag at your soul and push you further from the truth than you ever thought possible. You begin believing you've sinned too much to open the Bible. You're too distant from God to pray. No one at church would accept you, so why go? You start to seek that joy and peace in earthly pleasures.

The hangout sessions with your friend bring you some happiness, but when they leave, you're left with the lies still circling in your mind. You throw yourself into distractions to feel the way you did before you stopped reading the Word, but it only gives you sparks of happiness. It makes you happy in the moment, but when the tv show is over, you go back to feeling alone. That's why rooting yourself in the Word of God is essential.

I constantly felt alone for most of my life — even in a crowded room. However...every time I opened my Bible, I felt surrounded by love. I didn't feel alone anymore, and I couldn't believe it. The more I dug in and studied those words, the more I was left with peace even through the chaos that would follow. Materials and love from others will not leave you with peace or joy that lasts — only God can.

But even once I embraced Bible reading, I didn't change completely. My outlook on life and how I started conducting myself were different. My friends at school had commented on it many times in the months following. However, there was still something missing:

I wasn't praying.

Prayer was a massive struggle for most of my life. I had always loved reading, so reading the Bible was no problem. I would devour long novels in hours and stay up until four in the morning almost every night reading on my phone. But I had always struggled with communication, which made prayer difficult and stressful.

The whole subject of prayer confused me. I didn't understand how to pray. I didn't know what to pray about. I was so terrified of doing something wrong that I avoided it entirely. I was too scared of looking stupid to ask anyone how to pray.

I was scared of it.
I avoided it.
I neglected it.

Looking back now, it makes no sense at all. Why be so adamant about ignoring God? It may have made no sense, but I was guilty of it. Wasn't He the One that stitched up my broken heart? Isn't He still holding me together now? Why was I running from Him?

I decided to give prayer a shot...
I would never learn if I didn't try.

The fantastic thing about prayer is that you don't have to say something like, "O Lord, thou art the holiest in all the earth. Teach mine heart to listen to thine words..." You can be real. You can just say, "Lord, You're so amazing, and I just want to be like You. Please help me. I need it."

You don't have to use King James English to speak to Him. You can talk to Him just like you would talk to your best friend.

You can speak to Him about whatever you want. Don't feel afraid to talk to Him.

You may feel like you have no one to talk to, but you're so wrong. You can always talk to Jesus, who understands completely what you're going through. He was beaten. He was mocked. He was humiliated. He was betrayed. He was emotionally and physically abused.

He knows exactly what you're going through. Go to Him about it. Talk to Him about what you're going through. The things you are terrified to say out loud. The things that keep you up at night.

When you need to talk about your feelings, go to Him. Whenever you're so overwhelmed that you can no longer keep everything inside, go to Him. Whenever you're feeling alone and hopeless, go to Him.

Like the old adage says,
"pray about it as much as you think about it."

Think of Hannah. "Her adversary also provoked her sore, for to make her fret" (1 Samuel 1:6). She was harassed repeatedly by Peninnah for not having children. Hannah herself was also devastated that she couldn't have children. She dealt with so much pain, but do you know what she did?

She went down to the temple of the Lord and prayed until she wept. She poured her heart out before the Lord, and do you know what happened? Her circumstances changed. She didn't complain about it to others. She didn't spend all her time thinking about how she wished it would change... she prayed about it.

She poured out all of that anger she was harboring. Any bitterness she had. Any resentment that was developing. She poured out everything before the Lord... and a blessing came out of it. Little baby Samuel.

Prayer is that powerful. But there's also something about prayer that we like to ignore: you don't always get what you ask for. We can't think of God as a magical genie whose sole purpose is to give us the desires of our hearts.

The heart is deceitful above all things (Jeremiah 17:9), so we don't need some things that we think we need. We don't think things through all the way. When we want something, we ask for it without thinking of the consequences or effects of getting it. But God knows what's best for us.

Maybe your circumstance doesn't change instantly, but that doesn't mean you need to give up. Never stop praying. Just because you don't get an immediate change doesn't mean He isn't working. He could be setting a course of events that would change your life forever.

There are two things we need to remember during times like this -- silence doesn't mean that God isn't there, and "no" is an answer too. Sometimes, it's not even a "no." It's a "not right now." And when it's a no, it's often because a "yes" would lead to regrets later in life.

When I was younger (and very foolish)... the few times I actually did pray. I prayed for many things that I praise God for NOT saying yes to. If He had just allowed a yes instead of saying no, I would be stuck in a situation that would be destructive to my spiritual life.

I wouldn't be the person I have become, and I most definitely wouldn't be writing this book. I would be stuck with someone who wouldn't help my spiritual growth; in fact, he would have killed it. Now that I understand why my tearful prayers weren't given a yes, I am so glad that I couldn't "persuade" Him.

Another thing we must realize is that prayers aren't always answered the way we want them to be. Using myself as an example, I was expecting a grand homecoming. One where I would be greeted with emotional apologies. A gathering of all the family where I would finally feel that love I was lacking.

But that's not how it happened. Years later, I realized that the answer wasn't the wholeness I sought. I would move out, and that would be the end of the situation. It wasn't the complete turnaround I was expecting, but it was what would free me of all the pain I was experiencing.

If you're not like I was and your prayer life isn't struggling, but you still find yourself feeling anxious, depressed, or nothing in your environment is changing, just remember that it's not your fault. Anxiety and depression aren't always signs of a struggling prayer life or a "lack of faith." That was the case for me, but that's not the case for everyone.

Some people actually have an imbalance of neurotransmitters in their brains. What they're feeling is real because those neurotransmitters (what we like to call "chemicals") are binding incorrectly to receptor sites, the neurotransmitter isn't binding to the receptor site at all, their brain isn't producing enough of those neurotransmitters, or the reuptake process is failing them, and they have too many of certain neurotransmitters. Those are just *a few* examples of how that can happen.

Dealing with anxiety, depression, or trauma effects doesn't mean that you're a "bad Christian." Keep pressing through. Find someone you trust to talk to. Don't hold it all in because that will only hurt you in the long run. Tell your pastor and/or their spouse, a youth leader, or anyone else you trust what you're experiencing; you don't have to suffer in silence.

If you are like me, and you will admit that your prayer life is struggling, don't feel alone. Prayer is so often overlooked and undervalued. Reading an exciting Bible story is often easy, but setting aside the time to pray to the One whose words you read is hard. I, myself, have had significant trouble with prayer.

I could easily read multiple chapters a day. Reading the Bible was easy, but praying was different. When I was finally able to pray, I would find myself saying the same things repeatedly and never really having an honest conversation.

That was what the problem boiled down to. I wasn't having a personal *conversation* with Him, so I wasn't developing a personal *relationship* with Him. It wasn't until I realized that I couldn't talk to God because I didn't know Him for myself that I started being able to really pray.

I realized...
How can you talk to someone you don't really know?

When you first meet someone, you have awkward conversations because you don't know who they are. They are strangers to you, so you don't know conversation topics that interest them. You don't understand how they communicate, so sometimes you can misunderstand what they are saying. The first few conversations can seem very forced and unnatural.

But as you get closer, the awkwardness fades. You develop the ability to talk to them about anything. You know conservation topics that pique their interest. You even know topics to avoid. The shell of awkwardness that surrounded you has broken down. It seems natural.

If you are struggling with prayer, you need to
ask yourself if you know God or know *of* Him.
It's hard to talk to someone when you don't know what to talk to
them about.

If you don't have a personal relationship with God, it makes prayer awkward. Invest time into your relationship with God, and you'll see your prayer life grow. I'm speaking from personal experience. Your prayers will go from "God, please do this for me" to praying for other people in addition to individual needs. It will grow to asking for direction instead of just possessions. Prayer has the power to change your situation, but only if you allow it to.

Prayer and reading my Bible changed how I felt about myself. This process didn't occur overnight. It took years to get over everything I was letting hold me back. Don't be so hard on yourself if you're not seeing the progress you want in only a week.

There is no "one-size-fits-all"
for recovery of any kind.
There is not one single method that suits everyone.

In college, I studied social work, and the biggest thing they tell you in any class you take is that you can't treat all clients with the same method; every person has a different background. Each client has different needs and will respond better to different treatments. Because of this, certain clients might react negatively to the same method that another person would respond positively to.

This applies here as well. Don't compare your progress to another's. It never ends well. You are you. Your process is *uniquely you*. There is no "one-size-fits-all" for trauma recovery, so it is okay if your journey looks slightly different.

Trauma does not always look like people expect it to. Everyone experiences trauma differently. If there was something that happened to you or you experienced/witnessed something, and it has impacted you so much that it causes distress in your day-to-day life... it's trauma.

It's okay to call it what it is.

The word "trauma" is not reserved just for extreme examples. Because of this way of thinking, I wouldn't seek help. I hadn't been kidnapped. I didn't experience war. I didn't witness a murder. I felt like the abuse I experienced wasn't trauma — because that's a lie people who are uneducated on the subject like to perpetuate.

Think of trauma like a suitcase. Some suitcases are packed to the brim. They require extra help zipping up. When they are zipped up, they threaten to burst at the seams. There are a lot of items in that suitcase. Other suitcases only contain one or two items. They can easily be zipped up. It's quick and easy; you're ready to go. But no matter if it's packed to the brim or barely contains one full item...

The suitcase is still a suitcase.
The number of items in the suitcase doesn't change
the fact that it is a suitcase.

In the same way... trauma is trauma. It doesn't matter how "disastrous" or "minimal" we make it out to be. Trauma doesn't look the same for everyone. It isn't experienced the same for everyone. But it's still okay to *call it what it is*.

Likewise, processing trauma and trauma recovery don't look the same for each person. Sometimes it involves crying, but for others, they may never shed a tear. Some people look to journaling thoughts, prayers, etc., while that method would never cross someone else's mind. Each experience brings forth a unique healing process.

You've now heard a portion of my story of how Jesus brought me out of my darkness and into His marvelous light. I was heading down a path of destruction and despair before He stepped in. He taught me so many things along the way; however... your story does not need to look exactly like mine.

It doesn't need to look like anyone else's.
You have your own testimony of how God brought you out.

CHAPTER SEVEN:
Tell Your Story

"Come and hear, all ye that fear God,
and I will declare what he hath done for my soul."
— Psalm 66:16 (KJV)

During my years of silence and suppressing my testimony (see chapter three), I had countless opportunities to share what God had done for me. God was still working on me (and He still is), but there was a vast difference between me as a twelve-year-old and me in high school. I didn't have it all together. I hadn't fully processed what happened to me or moved on to it (because I was still living it), but I had a hope that made it all okay.

And I could have shared that hope with my peers.

I remember one occurrence of this very happening vividly. Even years later, I regret not acting on it while I had the chance. I was sitting in AP Literature my senior year of high school, back in 2018. It was sixth period, and the class was discussing the soliloquy in the play *Hamlet* where Hamlet contemplates suicide – or at least the class (minus one kid) decided that's what it really meant.

The discussion led to a situation where I could have shared my testimony so easily, seeing as it fits perfectly into the topic. My teacher even asked about personal experiences, but I kept my mouth shut and didn't say anything.

There was an opportunity right in front of me to tell a classroom full of my peers what God did for me. Statistically, at least one other person in that room had similar experiences. That person needed me to speak up. They were depending on me.

I had an opportunity to tell a group of teenagers about how I was this broken, depressed, and hopeless person that was completely transformed into someone who had a new hope and felt the unconditional love I've always longed for. But I sat silent. I decided that my story wasn't really that big of a deal. In my head, it didn't matter enough to tell, even though I *knew* this was the perfect opportunity to tell it.

The conversation had turned into precisely what I went through, but I never spoke a word. I was so terrified of people knowing the truth that I sat there silently — completely missing out on the chance to witness to people who might have really needed it. I was also terrified others would think that what I went through "wasn't a big deal." I didn't want to face the opinion of others.

I was so mad at myself when I walked out of the class. It was apparently evident because Harrison asked me what was wrong. I knew that what I had to say could have been exactly what someone needed to hear, but I was too concerned about myself — my own pride — to do anything about it.

I was so afraid that others would start treating me differently from everyone else that I decided my personal feelings were more important than someone's eternity. I decided I was wrong about the situation and convinced myself that my story didn't matter. I hope you don't lock your testimony away for years as I did.

Don't place your comfort above another person's salvation.

*"How then shall they call on him in **whom they have not believed**? and how shall they believe in him **of whom they have not heard**? and how shall they hear** without a preacher?" Romans 10:14 (KJV)*

For years, I believed that my story was invalid because many people were worse off than me. Sure, I suffered through physical and mental abuse, but some people out there suffered through that *and more*. Some didn't even get the chance to survive.

Sure, I grew up feeling like I wasn't capable of being loved, but I found people who would love me — others still don't feel that love. I thought that my story wasn't valid since there were people out there with a more traumatic story than mine.

As I have learned from my husband, the problem with that thinking is that there will always be someone "worse off" than you. That doesn't mean that your pain isn't valid. That doesn't mean your story won't touch people.

It definitely doesn't mean that your story shouldn't be heard. Your story is unique, and only YOU can tell it. No one can understand your story the way you do; therefore, no one can say that yours "isn't that bad."

They didn't experience the pain you felt. They didn't see the things that you have seen. Your testimony is just as valid as everyone else's. Don't fall into the same lie I fell into, or you'll spend years avoiding a calling.

At the start of this book, you read a little about my story, but there is still so much more. My story is full of twists and turns. It's full of paths that lead to unpleasant surprises, and if I were given a chance to write my story, I never would have written it like this.

I would have written myself the perfect, very happy childhood I could only dream of having — the fantasy childhood I saw all my friends living out. I would have written in me having so many friends. I would have given myself an outgoing and bubbly personality. I wouldn't have written in all of the pain and trauma that I've been through.

I wouldn't have written in my story being forced into an awkward and introverted personality. I wouldn't have written that I would always feel alone. But that's the problem. I wouldn't have written the things that give me my unique testimony. I wouldn't have written the things I was forced to learn that shaped me into the person I am today.

I wouldn't have written in all the words and actions that morphed me into this person who is stronger than I give her credit for. I wouldn't have written in the ministry that only I can fulfill.

My point is that if it were up to us, we wouldn't have lived with our crazy experiences. We would have most certainly written them out. I'm so glad we don't hold the pen because we would leave out a powerful testimony if we did. Everyone has a testimony that is unique to them alone, and no one else can tell it the way they can.

No one knows every detail of your testimony like you do. No one can understand the pain you went through like you can, and no one can tell it as eloquently as you can. No one can string words together that touch the core of someone's soul the way you can when it comes to *your testimony* because no one else has experienced it. Only you.

But we must remember that our testimonies are only powerful through God. It is not about us. We must remember while telling our stories to keep Him at the center. *It's not all about us.* I wouldn't have been able to get through any of it without Him. My story is a story of pain, hopelessness, abuse, loneliness, and nothing but a road leading to destruction. However, because of Him…my story is also a story of a mercy I wasn't worthy of, a love that I thought I would never experience, a hope the world can't take away, a grace I didn't deserve, and a God who was there through the midst of it all. He was there.

In my darkness.
In my hopelessness.
In my sorrow.
In the shadows.

He was there through it all… and through *Him* I am an overcomer. My testimony is not meant to glorify me but shows all the glory He *deserves.* That even me, someone so broken and without hope, still has a seat at His table. I wasn't worth it. I didn't deserve it. But He saw it fit to transform me.

The more you run from your past and try to sweep it under the rug, the less you can enjoy what is happening in the present. The harder you work to hide your past, the less you really live in the present. Ultimately, we give up our present AND future to ensure that our past is never discovered… when really… we should be sharing it.

You have no idea how many lives you touch every day through Him. The cashier that you never fail to ask about their day. The old lady you smile and wave at every time you pass her house. The followers you have on Instagram when you post a Bible verse or a picture of your Bible. Your friend that's secretly been debating going to church because she's impressed by all the things you tell her about God. The family you've desperately been praying for because you want them to come back to God. All of them. You have an impact on those people and so many more. Don't sell yourself short — He has given you a ministry.

As my dear friend, Clayton Houston, once put way back in the days of youth class, "We've all been given a role to fulfill. That doesn't stop when we're at the grocery store... we might not all be called to be a pastor, but we're all called to have a ministry and be a witness."

You have a ministry, and your testimony is at the core of that ministry. It's one of your most powerful weapons. Use it diligently. Use it often. Don't hide it away. Don't let it get dusty.

This is something that can't be silent.

Your testimony can be the very thing that speaks life to someone who needs it so desperately. It needs to be shared. I have lived in the goodness of God. His true light was always shining in my life. Even when I didn't recognize it. Even when I refused to admit it. I have LIVED in the goodness of God. My circumstance doesn't change His goodness. He kept me through the darkest times in my life.

I don't get to dictate if He is good —
He is good regardless of what I am experiencing.

While my life so far would not have been a route I would choose for myself, it took me one step closer to Him and becoming the person He made me to be. It showed me that while some people can be monstrous, there are many very gentle souls in this world who can love with every fiber of their being. Though this world can seem to come at you with everything it can, there is Someone much stronger standing in your place to fight for you, and He has given us a sword that we can use whenever we need to.

Without the storms, I wouldn't have learned that I can trust in Him. Without experiencing chaos, I wouldn't know how sweet

His peace is. Without the loneliness, I wouldn't have known how great His presence is.

Our testimonies can change the world. *Not because of us,* but the One our testimonies glorify. It gives people hope that God can do the same thing for them. Don't spend your days wishing it away.

The most important thing is that you don't lock up your story. Your story is your testimony. There are many people out there who could relate to your story. Your testimony of how God brought you through reminds others that by God, they can pull through.

Don't be afraid to share about the goodness of Jesus. How He lifted you from an endless cycle of abuse, stopped generational curses in their track through you, and was there through all the sleepless nights crying in bed. Your story of recovery gives hope to others that they can also process and recover from their traumas.

Tell the story.
Never stop telling the story.

The best example I can think of within the Bible is Paul. Paul, at this time known as Saul, was infamous for his pursuit to end Christianity. He would drag Christians to prisons... sometimes breaking into their homes to do so (Acts 8:3).

*"As for Saul, he made havock of the church, **entering into every house**, and haling men and women committed them to prison."*
Acts 8:3 (KJV)

He asked for letters that granted him permission to wreak even more havoc on the church. He was actually on the way to persecute more people when he converted to believing in Jesus after God spoke to him on that road to Damascus (Acts 9:1-19). You would think someone with a rap sheet like that would brush his story under the rug, right? Wrong.

Paul boldly proclaimed the transformation that occurred in his life — Philippians 3:1-11; Galatians 1:13-24; Acts 22:1-21. He did not hide what God had done in his life because he was scared of what others would think. He didn't leave out parts of his testimony because they were messy.

He understood that his testimony gave him a ministry. He could tell people how crazy his life was when he found God and the transformation God worked in him. Of all people, you would expect someone who wanted to kill what he eventually became to hide his story... but he didn't. He understood the power of a testimony (Revelation 12:11).

Don't lock away your testimony. You don't have to write a book. You don't have to post it for the world to see. But when you see someone struggling with something you struggled with, don't be afraid to tell them your testimony of hope. I hid my testimony for years and, in return, severely limited the witness that I could have had.

If all you read out of this book is these first few chapters,
please remember...
don't lock up your testimony.

CHAPTER EIGHT:
Bitterness and the Start of Restoration

*"Looking diligently lest any man fail of the grace of God; **lest
any root of bitterness springing up trouble you**, and thereby
many be defiled."*
— Hebrews 12:15 (KJV)

During high school, the physical abuse grew in intensity. I
was left even more broken after each blow. It hurt a lot more. Most
of the abuse I experienced during this time stemmed from lies
being told about me – blaming me for a mess, a broken plate, or
anything else someone didn't want to get the blame for. Where it
would have been fine if someone else made a mistake and broke a
plate, I would be beaten for doing the same thing.

Some of those living in my house found my abuse amusing
or thought that if it happened to me, it wouldn't happen to them; as
a result, sometimes, I was purposely lied on so that they could
watch and laugh at the abuse that would unfold. If I was ever
"tattled" on, it would result in hours of being screamed at, things
being thrown at me, and someone laying hands on me. Every.
Single. Time.

One day, my younger sister and I started fighting over a
chair. You know how you like to claim a "seat" when you're a kid
and not allow any of your siblings to sit there? Well, my dad had
this unbelievably comfortable recliner that he always sat in.

I was not allowed to sit in this recliner; it was reserved only
for him. He would even go as far as to refer to it as his "throne."
Anytime I tried to sit in it, I was immediately told to get up. My
younger sister, however, got a pass. One day, my sister claimed the
chair as her seat, and I used the typical response kids give, "it's not
your seat — I don't see your name written on it." I waited for her
to get up to get a drink, and then I stole the seat from her. I'll
admit... not the most amicable move. However, my dad was in his
room... so it was one of the few times I could get away with it. At
the time, I thought I needed to take the opportunity while it was
still there.

As she always did at this age, she ran to tattle on me. This time I was determined to stand up for myself. I refused to move — calling out the apparent favoritism. Big mistake. I was forced to get up. I usually wasn't very mouthy in my kid and teenage years because I was absolutely terrified of my parents. On a typical day, I would just give up and go to my room to sulk.

This day…
that was not the case.

I was growing very tired of being treated differently. I was tired of the favoritism and special treatment. As I said, I was determined to stand up for myself. I didn't foresee what would happen next; after all, it was a silly argument over a silly chair. This silly argument led to an intense episode of physical abuse. I was slapped. I was spit on. I was choked. While I was being choked, my vision started to get blurry. I was worried that the last thing I would see was my dad's angry, contorted face. But I was ready to go. I made my peace with God, fearing that this was really the end. I expected that to be my last thought. I was ready.

But my dad let go just in time.
I was shocked.
He threatened my life before he started choking me,
and I fully believed he would act on that threat.

What didn't help was that the rest of my family (minus my older sister, who was married and moved out at this point) looked on and did nothing. I couldn't blame them — what would stop him from doing the same to them if they said something? They were probably as scared as I was.

At this point, I was done. I had endured extreme abuse for a long time, but it was never this bad. I never thought my life was *actually* in danger. I know it was wrong in the eyes of the law, but I ran away. I ran (literally) away. I ran as fast as I could. My heart was pounding so hard that I could hear it in my ears.

All I could hear was the sound of my feet hitting the concrete and my heart pounding in my ears. It was a blessing from

God that I was still wearing shoes because my dad was right behind me in the truck. He wanted to save face and cover up what he did… probably already coming up with a cover story. He followed me along the way, trying to put out the fire before it spread.

I ran to a close friend's house, and her parents called the police… as they should have. I sobbed uncontrollably while I attempted to communicate the story as clearly as I could. Her parents were gentle and didn't rush me as I described the horrific scene that just happened while we waited for a police officer to arrive.

When the police officer finally arrived, I began to tell him my story. The expression on his face should have given away how this story would end away, but I still had hope as I started to explain what happened. He showed little patience, telling me that I needed to stop crying because there was no way that he would be able to understand me. He showed no empathy and it felt like all he cared about was getting this "whole ordeal" (as he put it) over with.

He interrupted me throughout the whole story to ask very pointed questions and concluded that I was rebellious teen trying to run away before I could complete the story. When I finished, his word shattered me. He didn't believe me.

When my friend jumped to defend me, citing the marks on my neck and face, he said… "She made them herself." When the words left his mouth, they quickly made a home in my mind. I internalized them.

A police officer… someone who I was supposed to trust would keep me safe had just told me that he didn't believe anything I had to say.

He even blamed me for the marks that were on my body. He accused me of doing it to myself to make up evidence. Her dad refused to let that be the conclusion. He reminded the officer of how my dad pulled into the driveway screaming that I couldn't prove anything.

"If he didn't do anything, why was he saying that?" her dad asked.

In that moment, I realized a life-shattering truth. Her dad was advocating for me and trying to protect me more than my own family ever had throughout my entire life. A person who didn't know much about me outside of the snacks I like to eat after school, that his daughter and I had the same favorite television show, and that I came from an abusive household was showing me more love and care for me than my own parents.

Another life-shattering truth was that the police officer didn't believe me. I always imagined when I finally told a professional, they would believe me, and advocate for me as much as the father of my friend did. But now, all I could think was that if a cop didn't believe me... who would? What was the point in telling anyone the next time I thought I was going to die from the abuse I was experiencing? Would *anyone* ever believe me?

When he left my friend's house and went to my house, he was fed lies. Like I suspected, he thought of a cover story and everyone in the house lied for him.

No report of the abuse was made. No one made any attempt to free me from the house I was being abused in.

It was then that I knew any chance of being rescued was lost. It was back to my prison after that day, where things would get much worse. Unbelievably worse.

After this day, I gave up seeking help I thought all hope was gone when the police officer walked out of the door. Why try to fight for myself? Why try to get help? Everyone else would blame me as well. Maybe it really was all my fault?

That thought consumed me.

I gave up on the idea of deliverance...
until a meeting with God on the
Redfield, Arkansas campgrounds.

I've always loved going to church camp. The presence of God was always so sweet; you could feel it in the air. With two services a day and constantly being surrounded by like-minded people, I would look forward to it all school year long.

During one altar call after the evening service, I began pouring my heart out to God. I knew it was something Hannah did in the Bible, so I decided to try it myself.

As I mentioned earlier, Hannah was relentlessly harassed by Peninnah for being barren. There was so much pain that she needed to work through, and she decided to give it to God. Everything turned out alright for her, so I thought it might for me as well.

So that was precisely what I did. I poured out my heart. I didn't worry about looking dignified. For the first time in a while, I didn't care what others thought of me. I needed this experience. At the time, I thought that all I had to do was pour my heart out, forgive, and never think about it again. I would receive the deliverance I was seeking and would never have to give my situation a second thought.

> I received the assurance that
> God would deliver me.
> But sadly, I went about it all wrong.

I manipulated this promise of deliverance and made it out to be what *I wanted it to be*. There was a man in the Bible who did something very similar. Naaman was a high-ranking individual — captain of the Syrian army. The Bible described him as "honorable" and as a "mighty man of valor" (2 Kings 5:1). A verse later, it goes on to say, "but he was a leper" (2 Kings 5:1). He had one thing that was plaguing him — one thing that he wanted deliverance from.

He sought the help of Elisha after a revelation about who he was (and the God he served) from his young maid. When he approaches Elisha, he is expecting a big miracle; he is expecting it to be made into a big spectacle. 2 Kings 5:11 documents him saying:

"behold, I thought, he will surely come out to me,
and stand, and call on the name of the Lord his God, and recover
the leper." (KJV)

Naaman wanted to be special, and he wanted an extraordinary
miracle.

He almost missed his miracle because it didn't meet *his* expectations. I hope that is never said of me, but it almost was. You see, every camp after that would be a reminder that my promise still hadn't come. I would pour my heart out all over again, but nothing ever seemed to happen.

Every year, I would still go home to living in constant fear and dwelling in brokenness. Some years, I would go home to a situation worse than when I left it for camp. There was not a happily ever after in sight — no end to my pain and suffering. I was getting desperate, and I needed a way out.

I was ready to take God's promise into my own hands.

I'll go into more detail in the next chapter, but my promise didn't come as I expected or wanted it to. My deliverance did not come (immediately) in the form of restoration as I had hoped. It came as a rescue. A month after my final year of senior camp, I was rescued in a way I never dreamed possible.

During this waiting period, I became very bitter... without even noticing. I was unknowingly walking straight down a path of bitterness and unforgiveness. All while blissfully — and mostly ignorantly — thinking I was justified in all my actions. I thought it would give me more satisfaction to refuse to forgive, but it really left me even more broken and longing for what I didn't have.

I didn't realize that deeper issues were going on under the surface. What I thought was a justified reaction was really an unhealthy coping mechanism in disguise. I chose bitterness because bitterness doesn't require working through the pain. Bitterness allows us to avoid pain. And that's why it's so easy to choose over forgiveness.

I couldn't bear to face the pain, so I chose the route that led to bitterness. Rather than getting better, I got bitter. I hated them. To be blunt, sometimes I wished they would die so the abuse would stop. And if they had died, I wouldn't have cried. That sounds awful, doesn't it?

But that is the truth, and I promised myself that I would be completely transparent in this book. I couldn't stand them. They did so much to me. They took so much from me.

Forgive them?
I could never.

But the problem with choosing the route of bitterness instead of healing is that bitterness develops strong roots. The Bible warns us to watch out for the root of bitterness (Hebrews 12:15).

*"Follow peace with all men, and holiness, without which no man shall see the Lord: looking diligently lest any man fail the grace of God; **lest any root of bitterness springing up trouble you, and therefore many be defiled.**"*
Hebrews 12:14-15 (KJV)

Why?

Bitterness can creep into our lives unbeknownst
to us and steal more and more ground...
slowly choking out fruits we should bear like
longsuffering, patience, and gentleness (Galatians 5:22-23).

I love plants. I have over twenty plants in my house as I'm typing this — and probably a lot more by this book's publication. What has shocked me the most about starting to keep plants is how fast roots can grow. I've gotten exceptionally acquainted with propagating pothos plants.

When propagating a pothos, I cut off a stem a little below a node (the connecting point of leaf and stem) and place it in a glass jar full of water. It always amazes me how quickly a root will shoot out of the node. In no time, the glass jar I placed it in is full of roots shooting out in every direction; the plant is ready to be moved to soil.

> In the right conditions,
> roots can grow quicker than we may expect.
> It's the same with bitterness.

It can quickly take hold of more and more of our hearts. It starts out with roots that stay in their designated place. We think we have it under control, but it quickly overtakes more and more ground. That's why I didn't notice it even happening to me.

If we're not careful, we can let it overtake us. If you let it continue to take root and become overgrown, it can choke out the good things in life. In the end, it does more damage to you than to those who have hurt you.

We have to uproot it as soon as we notice signs of it. We must forgive, even when there is no apology. Even when they don't seem to show any remorse at all. If we don't, bitterness will creep into our hearts and slowly take over. The root of bitterness kills our pursuit of holiness and walking after Him.

It can happen without us even realizing it, as it did with me. Bitterness was holding me hostage, demanding a ransom only God could pay. But it wasn't always that way. It crept up on me. I didn't even realize how bitter I was getting.

We must be proactive in stopping the process. I would laugh when people said we should forgive because "they didn't know what happened to me." But that was just another cry for help. It was another sign that I had been overtaken by bitterness.

My heart had become so hardened toward them that I had no empathy for them. I didn't realize that they were human too. As ashamed as I am to admit this, I failed to recognize that they had a soul…I stopped caring about where their souls would go if they passed from this life.

That was the biggest red flag that I had a severe bitterness problem. If you think you have honestly moved on and forgiven people, ask yourself that question: would I still try to lead them to God so their souls would be saved? Suppressing all of my feelings under the guise that I was justified in holding back my forgiveness led me to develop these feelings.

Like me, Jonah had to learn this lesson the hard way. If you follow his story, he is called to preach to Nineveh (Jonah 1:2). Jonah… deciding for himself who deserves forgiveness… ran from the call (Jonah 1:3) and went to the city of Tarshish instead.

To make a long story short, Jonah ends up in Nineveh… the exact place he was running from. And Jonah, not having fully learned his lesson, pouts about it. He does not like the fact that God is willing to forgive Nineveh:

"But it [God forgiving and showing mercy to Nineveh] *displeased Jonah, and he was very angry. And he prayed unto the Lord, and said, I pray thee, O Lord, was not this my saying, when I was yet in my country? Therefore I fled before unto Tarshish: **for I knew that thou art a gracious God, and merciful, slow to anger, and of great kindness, and repentest thee of evil.** Therefore now, O Lord, take, I beseech thee, **my life from me; For it is better for me to die than to live."** Jonah 4:1-3 (KJV)*

Jonah was willing to let thousands of people die because he was biased against them -- he didn't see any value in them. They wouldn't be given a second chance if it were up to Jonah. Jonah *should have* felt sorry for the 12,000 people living in spiritual darkness and hoped for their salvation.

He fled from Nineveh because he *knew* his God was a God of second chances… and he didn't like that. To Jonah… they didn't deserve a second chance. Jonah got his second chance in Jonah 3:1, but he wasn't okay with the people of Nineveh getting one.

Not only did he throw a fit when Nineveh got a second chance, he cared more when a gourd died than he did when there was a possibility of thousands of human beings dying:

*"And then the Lord prepared a gourd, and made it to come up over Jonah… **So Jonah was exceedingly glad of the gourd…** and it came to pass when the sun did arise, that God prepared a*

80

*vehement east win; and the sun beat upon the head of Jonah... and [Jonah] **wished in himself to die.**" Jonah 4:6-8 (KJV)*

Don't get me wrong, I love plants just as much -- if not more -- than the next person... just look at my house. But I don't get happier over a plant than I do the salvation of 12,000 people. He was so upset with God's mercy and compassion toward the people of Nineveh. God wanted Jonah to understand that if Jonah could be upset over a plant (that he didn't even cause to grow) shouldn't God care about His creation? Living and breathing people?

Jonah was in great need of checking his priorities.
And if we're honest with ourselves...
We do too.

If we can't rejoice if the people who hurt us come to the Lord... we have a serious problem. If we place more importance on the hurt and feeling justified than we do on their soul... we have a severe problem.

My advice for those dealing with bitterness is don't bury your feelings. Recognize them, acknowledge them, but don't focus so much on getting closure that you don't allow yourself to move on. We won't always get the closure we're seeking.

We won't always get the apology we've been waiting for, but we can't allow this to keep us from moving on or starting new. Bitterness thrives in darkness — in the places we think are hidden away from everyone, where its roots reach deeper than we may realize. Soon taking over.

It's essential to understand the cycle:
unforgiveness gives root to bitterness,
bitterness gives root to resentment,
resentment gives root to hatred.

This is why we must cut it off at the source —
forgive regardless, without needing an apology.
Or even a sign of remorse.

Harboring a spirit of unforgiveness is like a tapeworm to your soul. Tapeworms physically cannot digest their own food as they have no digestive tract. To combat this, they steal food already processed by another organism. It steals all the nutrients that the organism worked so hard to digest. If we're not careful, that spirit of unforgiveness can latch onto our hearts and rob us of all the fruits (Galatians 5:22-23) we've worked so tirelessly to develop. It can rob us of our peace. Our patience. Our gentleness.

The more we allow it to grow,
the more it steals from us.

"For my yoke is easy, and my burden is light"'
Matthew 11:30 (KJV)

The yoke of bitterness is heavy, but we don't have to let it weigh us down. The yoke of hatred can be unbearable, but it was never something we should have placed on ourselves in the first place. It was never something that we were intended to take on and bear.

We can't allow bitterness to grow in our garden because it will steal nutrients from other fruits we try to cultivate. We are called to love our enemies and even pray for them. Use that time to ask that He help you forgive. Freely. Without holding back.

The ultimate cure to bitterness is love.

*"But **love your enemies**, and do good, and lend, expecting nothing in return, and your reward will be great, and you will be sons of the Most High, **for he is kind to the ungrateful and the evil**."*
Luke 6:35 (ESV)

How do you learn to love someone who has hurt you? How do you model the same love that God gives us? Learning to love someone who hurt you is hard. It takes time. It takes patience. Strength. Humility. And so much more.

But the beautiful truth of the process is that we don't have to do it alone. When we don't feel like we're strong enough, we can lean on the strength of God. When we feel like we're running out of patience, we can ask Him to help us cultivate more.

Through my experience with my family, I realized there are six practical steps to developing that love:
1. Pray for them
    a. Pray that they develop a personal relationship with God
    b. Pray that they come to a place of repentance
    c. Pray that they learn to forgive themselves
    d. Pray that God blesses them even when you don't feel like they should be blessed (Romans 12:14)
2. Pray for your own mind
    a. Pray that you will come to a place of true forgiveness
    b. Pray that you will gain (and embrace) peace
    c. Pray that your mind will be protected from any harmful words directed at you
    d. Pray for wisdom in your words and actions
    e. Pray that you will turn to God during times of hurt
3. Practice empathy and compassion
    a. Humanize them in your mind – recognize that they might be just as broken as you are and that they are human too.
    b. Don't stoop to their level
    c. Place yourself in their shoes – try to understand where they're coming from (this isn't excusing what they did, but trying to understand where it might stem from)
4. Create healthy boundaries
    a. Boundaries set the standard for how you will allow others to treat you
    b. Forgive and love, but don't put yourself back into an environment or relationship that is not safe for you
    c. Make sure that you are reinforcing those boundaries

5. Start the process of forgiveness
   a. It's a conscious choice that you must make daily
   b. Some days will be easier than others… but stick with it
   c. Forgiveness doesn't mean that you are excusing what they did
   d. It's for your own good… it frees you
6. Give yourself time
   a. Don't compare your journey to another
   b. It's a process… it (without divine intervention) won't happen overnight
   c. Don't push yourself to do anything before you're ready… this can hinder the process
   d. Healing IS possible (Psalm 147:3; James 5:16; Philippians 4:19; Psalm 107:20; Psalm 30:2; Matthew 9:35)

These are just some steps that I learned along the way that helped me choose love instead of bitterness. They are simple but are helpful if you don't know where to start. Remember, it might not seem like it while you're in the moment but choosing love over bitterness will always be best for you in the long run. Make sure bitterness isn't growing in your garden.

I always check my garden to see what's growing every now and then. I want to see empathy, love, and forgiveness each time, as I let bitterness grow for far too long.

Letting go is truly freeing.
You can feel it too.

CHAPTER NINE:
The Truth and Lies About
BROKENNESS

*"**Those who sow in tears shall reap with shouts of joy**! He
who goes out weeping, bearing the seed for sowing, **shall
come home with shouts of joy**,
bringing his sheaves with him.."*
— *Psalm 126:5-6 (ESV)*

I never had much support during high school. I was
dropped off at my band concerts. While everyone else had their
parents rooting for them in the crowds, I was alone. No one was
cheering me on. Seeing parents taking pictures with their kids to
post how proud they were of them later ate away at me.

In band, All-Region band is one of the top
accomplishments (or at least it was in my area). You receive and
have to learn to play four to five sheets of music that would be
complex for the high school level. You have to sight-read (play for
the first time without ever practicing it before) a sheet of music
they pick out that you've never seen before. You also have to
memorize all your scales because they will require you to play a
few random scales in addition to the prepared music and sight-
reading portion.

You spend months practicing it, and in January — you
audition. They also don't tell you which pieces of music they will
make you play from the prepared selection, so you just hope they
choose the few you're best at.

It takes a lot of time, determination, and dedication. I
would spend almost 500 minutes a week practicing for it. As a
result, I made the All-Region band every year I tried out. You
would think that my parents would love to take me to those to at
least just show off... but they didn't.

They would, as always, drop me off and pick me up when I
texted them. My senior year — arguably the most important one of
all — Harrison and his grandmother had to take me because they

refused to. It was the first time I was excited to go; someone would finally be watching from the crowds. Harrison also brought me flowers; I don't think he will ever understand how much that small, simple gesture really meant to me.

I also grew up accepting awards... important awards... on my own. When I was chosen to be one of three seniors of my school nominated for an award recognizing outstanding students, my parents weren't there. This time, Harrison and *his* father had to take me.

I accepted so many awards that I was so proud of alone. No one (aside from a school photographer) would be there to capture the moment. I wouldn't get a post later on about how proud my parents were of me, as most of my friends' parents did. I received little to no support from them.

For my graduation, my parents weren't going to go. My nana somehow talked my parents into letting her take my siblings to watch. I was almost alone... on graduation day. The most important day of my high school career. This lack of support added to the source of my bitterness toward them.

This drastically changed after I started dating Harrison. By the end of high school, I finally had support. Harrison's family had taken me in and supported me in anything I did. They became my step-in family — the family that chose me. Harrison supported me and pushed me to do the things I was scared to try. I even finally had supportive friends.

I finally felt an acceptance I only dreamed I would feel... but I wasn't used to it. The love and support... just felt so foreign to me. I couldn't understand how to accept this love. And I sometimes struggle with this to this day. Harrison was getting too close. His family was way too nice. I started pushing them all away. I didn't want to get too attached and then lose what I had with all of them. I grew distant.

What was the point? I didn't try to get to know any of them. At home, my parents told me that Harrison would eventually get tired of me and leave me. I didn't believe them at first, but you can only hear something for so long before you start to believe it.

So I distanced myself. And I've regretted it ever since. Pushing people away has always been my way of coping when it felt like people were getting too close to the truth. They couldn't know. If a cop couldn't even believe me, I stood no chance of anyone else believing me. Why try to make connections when they would be ripped apart sooner or later? I found myself clinging to the lies I was being told instead of trusting the truth Harrison was giving me.

He loved me.
He really did.
His family cared about me.
They really did.

But I couldn't believe it. Who could love me? As I explained earlier, I was convinced I was unlovable at this point in my life. *How* could they love me? How could *anyone* possibly love me?

The people I loved more than anyone else in this world... the people who I still adored despite all they had done to me... the people I longed would love me... didn't. I would cry night after night, wondering why I wasn't enough for them. What was wrong with me? How could *anyone* possibly love me?

For this reason, I didn't trust Harrison's stability. I didn't believe that he would actually stay like he promised. He would talk about our future, and I couldn't let myself get excited... that would only hurt more when he inevitably left me. But I was wrong. He did love me. He has for a while.

Are you still clinging to the lies you were told? The names you were called? The experiences you didn't ask for? Are you letting those become your identity? Sometimes I find myself still believing the names I was called. Sometimes I can still hear their voices when I go to do something — whether for the very first time or the one-hundredth time.

Occasionally when I go to sing a solo, all I can hear is, "is something killing a cat? Because that's what it sounds like." A "joke" that never failed to follow me singing. When I go to draw something just for fun, I can't block out... "you'll never be good, so there's no point in trying." When Harrison and I are on a date, the idea that he doesn't actually love me, that he's with me out of pity, or he will eventually get tired of me still lingers… it screams at me. That's all they would say about our relationship until a month before we got engaged. When I go to do anything out of my comfort zone, it's like they're still there, ready to throw insults at me.

The thing is, I know that these things aren't true. I know that nothing they would insult me with was true. I can recognize that in my brain. But the never-ending echo of their voices makes it harder to remember what they're saying isn't true. When you experience this, the best thing to do is look at the Word. God can't lie. He can't sin. If He were to lie, He wouldn't be God. So everything He's ever said about you is true.

The Bible is full of things that God thinks of us. It's full of promises. It's full of not only the identity we should bear as Christians— but, more importantly — His identity. If you're struggling to fight the lies you've heard for years, find the truth in His word. If the voices in your head don't line up with it, it *cannot* be true. And while you're there, take some time to remind yourself of the characteristics of God. Remind yourself that you can rest in the arms of a loving God. One who has many loving thoughts toward us. His opinion is the one that matters most.

We need to stop letting ourselves believe
the lies we were fed.

* * *

The care that they had for me — Harrison's entire family — became a lot more real to me when his grandmother offered to let me live with her. I was getting out… *finally*. After years of hoping and waiting, my promise was finally being fulfilled. It wasn't how I expected or wanted it to be, but it was much better.

What I didn't know was that this rescue allowed me to spend a few years growing closer to someone I would only have a few more years with. At the time, I didn't know that just a few months later, his grandmother's health would start to deteriorate… and I would need to help her more than I realized. The move that allowed her to be there for me turned into a situation that allowed me to be there for her.

It seems like perfect timing looking back on it now. But at the time… I felt really guilty. I was leaving behind all of my younger siblings. They were safe from physical harm, especially my two sisters who are on the spectrum. The only person who was in danger physically at the time was me, but I was the one raising them.

I was changing the diapers. Most days, I was cooking the food (or heating up pizza rolls). I was cleaning the house. I was running a household all on my own. After my older sister moved out when I was fifteen, I no longer had her help — I was doing it all alone.

I felt guilty. I was worried about them from a neglect standpoint, but I was being abused in basically every definition of the word. My mental health was deteriorating. Some days I couldn't even get out of bed. I was losing weight from stress, and I was already severely underweight. It was the hardest decision I've ever made. I felt like I was abandoning my sisters.

But once again, God proved to me that He really is the best problem solver. My parents seemed to keep getting financial blessings after I moved out. This significantly reduced my fears of them not having enough food to eat. A few family friends started hanging around. Ones that I could trust. They would hold my parents accountable for taking care of the girls. It all seemed to be working out.

My rescue came.

I was reminded once again of the goodness of God. This rescue proved that I could trust in His timing… that His promises never fail. The difference between this new house and my old house was astronomical. It was so quiet. I didn't have to worry about what I said. My mind was not consumed with the fear of what happened next.

For my first couple of months… I was actually a little uneasy with how peaceful everything was. I was waiting for the minute it would all change. During this time, I still felt like I was unlovable. I was waiting for the moment Granny would realize why no one else wanted me around. There had to be something wrong with me. I was always told I was the problem.

Shortly after I had moved in with Harrison's grandmother, my parents (who had no idea that I would actually start living there) showed up, dropped off all of my stuff in her yard, and told me I wasn't welcome home anymore. I panicked. I didn't want his grandmother to know what they were doing, so I quickly tried to move everything inside before she could notice. Harrison's younger cousins were also there at the time, and I definitely didn't want them exposed to what was happening.

I just told her that it was all of my winter clothes. I moved in during the middle of July, which happened around August. It made sense that I would need clothes for the cooler months. My deception worked. But I was sent back into feeling like I did when I lived in my old house. I escaped the physical abuse, but the neglect lingered. Somehow even though I was out of the house, they still found a way to get to me.

I was kicked out at eighteen. My parents discarded my clothes and a few possessions in the yard. With that single act, they cut all ties with me. My sister texted me later to tell me that they were now saying that they were "disowning me."

I was no longer a part of the family.

I was now tossed away like I didn't matter. No one wanted me. This feeling only grew, and I started to feel like the McCall's only took me in because they felt sorry for me... including Harrison. That was far from the truth, but my trauma kept telling me otherwise.

My parents didn't know that I was going to *live* with Granny. To keep them from blowing up and causing a scene, they were under the impression that I would stay for a few weeks to help Granny.

When they dropped off my belongings on the curb, they didn't know I had a place to stay until Harrison and I married. For all they knew, after the few weeks were over... I would be returning to live with them. Them kicking me out meant that I would be living on the street. They didn't care... and that broke me. I always thought that someday they would come around. As time went on, I lost more and more of that hope. That day destroyed what little hope I had left.

I was only eighteen.
Used, abused, and discarded.

I was hopeless again. Grieving the loss of my parents, and they were still alive. My brokenness started consuming me. I was in a better place physically, but my mental state was worse than ever. I was safe physically, but wars were still being waged in my mind.

My family was torturing me without even being in the same house as me. To me, it was even worse that they could still have such an impact on me while being miles away. The distance didn't stop the threatening texts. The Facebook posts trashing me to the whole world. They weren't there with me, but they were still wreaking havoc in my life.

As I said, I was being consumed with my brokenness... but I didn't realize how broken I was becoming by harboring things in my heart that didn't belong there. Sometimes we don't realize how broken we are until God starts working on us. We don't realize that the pieces we thought were so strong are actually shattered until He starts mending them. Sometimes, it takes Him putting the pieces back together before we realize how many pieces there really were. Some that we didn't even realize we could have.

When God starts working on us, sometimes past hurts you didn't realize were affecting you rise to the surface. It's important to not stifle this. Don't push them back down. The worst that we can do is ignore the pain. This will only stunt our healing process. Talk to God and others you trust (a friend, a therapist, a pastor) about the hurt.

Journal about your pain. The thing that got me through so much was journaling. I journaled prayers about the process. I journaled feelings in a place where I could express my unfiltered thoughts. I talked to God because I knew that anything I told Him was safe with Him.

The most important thing I learned during this time was that I didn't have to stay that way; I didn't have to stay broken. My brokenness was not too much to handle, even though I had been told otherwise. But the idea of no longer being broken was foreign to me. This leads me to a topic I feel we don't talk about enough. We talk about trauma and the effects of it...but not the impact of trauma recovery.

That probably doesn't make sense to you, but hear me out. When I no longer felt broken or helpless, I got scared. When God healed me from a long list of mental health issues and the impact years of abuse and neglect had on me...I was confused.

For so long, I had been that broken person. I had been severely depressed with no hope at all. I was that super anxious person who was always on edge because I had to expect anything that came my way. I lived life looking for the next bad thing that would happened because that was all I knew.

But most of all…
people just treated me like I was a normal person
because no one knew.

The entire start of my new life (where I was more open and honest about what I had endured) was lived in the shell of protection. People treated me like I was made of glass. People would become very cautious around me. They would trip over themselves, avoiding certain words once they figured out what my childhood (and teen years) were really like. As a result, it felt scary to step out of the brokenness.

I didn't want people to treat me any differently. I was so comfortable being broken that it was scary when God made me whole. We need to allow ourselves to live in the freedom that Christ bought us. It's okay to feel a little uncomfortable at first, but we can't stop God's work. I did so many times, and I wish I had known that it's not as scary as I thought it was.

Don't let this fear keep you from telling your story. Yes, some people will treat you differently. Most people won't. Most people will see your strength in your story -- not your weakness. It's okay to be scared, but we can't let that hinder us.

I don't speak about abuse often because I always get scared of the reaction, but it is a huge part of my testimony. We can't hold back the details of our testimonies just because it isn't pretty.

Speak your story.
Allow God to mend the brokenness.
Your brokenness does not separate you from God.

During this time, I also learned that my brokenness and trauma did not disqualify me from whatever God had planned for me. Being broken doesn't disqualify you from being used by God. Coming from a broken family doesn't disqualify you from being used by God. There is no form of brokenness that is too much for God to use. I learned that if it's something you can continue to glorify God through, it can't possibly damage any ministry you have.

In my weakness, I can boast about the saving strength of the Lord. In overcoming the darkest days, we can shine His beacon of hope. If it gives me a chance to share about God's goodness, then it can never disqualify me from whatever potential ministry I might have.

Brokenness does not separate us from God. It also doesn't limit what you can do for the Kingdom. Every winding road that led to disappointment He was still there. He was still working. Even when I couldn't recognize God's hand in my life at the time. Even when I didn't see how He was using every hurt... every bump in the road... for His good. He never let it go to waste. My disappointment wasn't for nothing. My pain wasn't for nothing. Every experience led me to God.

When I was stripped of all my hope, I searched for something to find hope in. I tried many different things, but nothing worked. I tried romance...and that didn't work. I tried friends...and that didn't work. I would get so absorbed in watching movies to distract myself, but nothing truly helped. The feeling was always still there. The search for hope led me to God. I didn't go out searching for God. I wasn't consciously trying to find Him. But when I searched for hope, I (of course) found it in the God of hope (Romans 15:13).

Along the way, I learned what it was like to truly depend on God. He made ways for me that I knew could never have been made by anything else. Dealing with trauma helped me learn to trust in Him because I couldn't trust in anything else. All the storms really just drove me to Him. Like the song says, He took all that was meant for evil and turned it for my good.

When I tell people my story, one of the first things they ask me is how I managed to not be angry at God. Some people will even offer up stories similar to mine where the person turned from God for the rest of their life. There's nothing special about *me* that made it possible for me to turn to God during the storm where others ran away.

Trauma doesn't have to drive a wedge between you and God. That's a comment people will often say — they don't know how to trust God when people in their life are so unreliable. God isn't like us. It's against His nature to be unreliable. He's with us everywhere we go. During everything we experience.

He's constant.
Unwavering.
Immovable.

He promises over and over again through His Word that He will never abandon us (Deuteronomy 31:6; Psalm 94:14; Joshua 1:5). If there is anyone you can trust, it's Him.

Don't allow yourself to be consumed by your brokenness.
Don't allow that brokenness to separate you from God.

CHAPTER TEN:
You Are Not Your Family Tree

*"Therefore if any man be in Christ, **he is a new creature**: old things are passed away; behold, all things are become new."*
— *2 Corinthians 5:17 (KJV)*

For the few years of my life, I accepted what was my normal to be the trajectory for the rest of my life. College? Impossible. No one else in my family went. A healthy, God-centered marriage? Impossible. No marriage in my family has ever been like that. A home that is safe and free from drugs and alcohol? There are very few in my family without at least one of the two.

Sometimes we need to question our normal. God had so much more in store for me than I could have imagined at the time... and I was ready to give it all up just because I couldn't see it yet. After escaping my house, I was expecting an immediate healing. One day, I became so frustrated that I prayed a short prayer where I expressed how frustrated I was with my healing process. I felt like I should have been further along in my journey than where I currently found myself.

I spent *eighteen years* in a house that tarnished my mental health, and I was ready to give up all of my faith if I wasn't completely healed in a *five-minute prayer*. I fully believe people who say they were instantly healed of PTSD, anxiety, depression, or any other similar disorder. I believe them. But that instant healing isn't something that happens for everyone. A lot of the time, healing is a process. A short, medium, long, or anywhere-in-between kind of process.

I was willing to give up all my belief in God because I wasn't ready to go through the process. I wanted to heal, but I wasn't willing to put in any work. I wasn't willing to trust that the God of the process knew what He was doing. I wasn't willing to expose the deepest hurts in my life to anyone... not even God. I wanted a quick fix. I didn't want God to work on my heart.

I didn't want to consciously make
decisions to continue my healing process.

I was ready to accept that I would be like everyone else in my family. I decided that I could live with what I had and accept it as my normal. What I was experiencing was *learned helplessness*.

Learned helplessness is a psychological term for when a person feels powerless after experiencing something traumatic. When you've experienced a traumatic situation over and over, you start to believe there is nothing you can do to change the situation. You think you'll never have the strength or resources to change your outcome. That is learned helplessness.

And that's where I was living for those few years. I was going to be just like everyone else. My life would not make a difference. I would find myself in a loveless marriage with many children. We would be in poverty... just as I have always been. There would constantly be drugs cycling through my house.

I would be camped out between misery and acceptance of my miserable environment. I would always be teetering from one side to another... eventually a false sense of acceptance would fall over me. This is my life.

That is not my life.
It never had to be.

I am brought to tears when I realize how much God has done for me. Words can't express all God has worked in my life and my heart. I don't have to worry about being just like the rest of my family.

I don't have to be my family tree.

My school counselor and teachers heavily encouraged me to apply to college. Harrison and his family did as well. I didn't see much of a point... no one in my family would drive me to class. And even if they did, I couldn't afford it. One college semester tuition alone is upwards of $4,000. That doesn't even include books. How could I possibly afford that?

To appease those encouraging me to apply, I did. To my shock, I got an acceptance letter. Blinded by my own insecurity, I never thought I would be "good enough" to get into college. Yet there I stood, holding an acceptance letter.

Then I got a Pell Grant *and* scholarships that guaranteed I never had to pay a penny of the tuition. In fact, I always got enough money back in a refund check that I never had to pay for my books myself either. My entire (undergraduate) college season was completely paid for. Even after my parents stole my graduation money. Even after I didn't do well on the ACT (I have never done well on timed tests).

The first day of college quickly rolled around, and I was ecstatic. This was the first day of my new life. I was already moved out of my house and into the house of Harrison's grandmother. I was ready to take on life.

But... old, uninvited guests have a way of rearing their ugly heads again. Even during a time that seems so happy and carefree.

During my years at college, my biggest struggle was accepting that God was calling me to things outside of my comfort zone. To be honest, they weren't just outside my comfort zone... they were in a whole new area code. Miles and miles away from my comfortable little bubble.

Sharing my story... was a terrifying idea.
I knew that this was what I needed to do though.
I could no longer deny the call.

But who would want to listen to the words of a girl born into brokenness? Who was raised in the ashes of her parents' broken dreams. Who bore the brunt of years of pent-up frustration. Who would want to listen to her?

I've always seen the look people gave me once they heard my last name. I knew that once they knew which branch of the family tree I came from... they instantly put up their guard. Before I spoke a word, they would place me in a box in their mind that I would have to fight to get out of. I thought that I would only ever be seen as the girl who was abused by her dysfunctional family for the rest of my life.

And who would want to listen to her?

Who would want to listen to the girl from a long line of people who weren't preachers, pastors, missionaries, or Sunday school teachers? Instead, I came from a long line of alcoholics, (hard) drug addicts, wife beaters, child abusers, and even people who participated in incest. My family tree is well known in my corner of Northeast Arkansas. In fact, the reputation even extends further to many other areas of Arkansas. People already have a negative perception of me just by realizing who I am related to.

I was surrounded by the worst possible influences
and heading down a road of destruction... but God.

He saw me. He heard me. He loves me. Through my many nights crying myself to sleep while talking to Him, I realized that the cycle of abuse can and will end with me. I didn't have to follow in their footsteps. I didn't have to act out everything I saw and heard. I realized that I could stop the cycle... through Him.

For years, I was terrified of becoming like them. I was worried I would end up treating Harrison the way I saw them treat each other. After all... that was all I knew. I was afraid I would slowly morph into their mini-me without realizing it. I was plagued with nightmares of me turning into my parents. I thought that something I could not control nullified any call that God had placed on me.

But I am not them. I am not my family tree. Neither are you. We don't have to stay in the cycle we are stuck in, or at least it seems we are stuck in. We serve a generational-curse-breaking God. That's one of the biggest lessons I've learned and still need to be reminded of.

With one word, chains that were holding us back for years crumble. At the mention of His name, all the things plaguing our families can vanish. Nothing can stand in His presence — everything must bow:

*"That at the name of Jesus **every knee should bow**,*
*of things **in heaven** and things **under the earth**;*
and that every tongue shall confess that Jesus Christ
is Lord, to the glory of God the Father."
Philippians 2:10-11 (KJV)

Nothing can stand in His presence. Not anxiety. Not generational curses. Not depression. Not our own expectations of what makes someone "qualified" for ministry.

To have a ministry, you don't have to be a Bible college graduate. You don't have to come from a squeaky-clean background to serve God and be used by Him. The call of God is not contingent on our talents or works. He doesn't need you to be *able*; he just needs you to be *willing*.

He doesn't require you to be an outstanding singer. He doesn't need you to be able to speak in front of a large crowd — if that were the case, I'm already disqualified. All He wants is a heart willing to say, "yes! Here I am."

Your background or family tree does not disqualify you. You are not responsible for the sins of your family. I carried around a weight that wasn't even mine for too long. It almost crushed me. It wasn't mine to bear, but I convinced myself it was my problem. I convinced myself that it disqualified me from everything. As stated earlier in this chapter, I didn't think anyone would want to listen to *me*.

I wasn't dedicated as a baby. I didn't grow up knowing the truth. I didn't grow up falling asleep under pews. I didn't scribble to my heart's content on a notepad from my mother's purse as the preacher preached his heart out. I did not grow up in church, and I don't have a squeaky-clean family tree.

But if you look at the Bible… you can find many examples of people who fulfilled roles and ministries that their relatives didn't. If you read the book of Amos, it makes it clear that Amos was not the son of a prophet but was called by God to be a prophet.

*"Then answered Amos, and said to Amaziah, **I am not a prophet, neither was I a prophet's son;** but I was an herdman, and a gatherer of sycamore fruit."*
Amos 7:14 (KJV)

God took him from the field and made him a prophet. This story reminds me of David, whom God brought out of his father's field and to be made a king. These serve as two great reminders that you don't have to come from a long line of preachers to be a preacher. You don't have to come from a line of prophets to be a prophet. You can act in roles regardless of the image of the family you came from.

God is not limited by your family tree.

If you look at the story of Mephibosheth (2 Samuel 4, 5, & 9), you can also see this at play. Mephibosheth was a genuinely nice guy... but also had a messed-up family tree. Mephibosheth was the son of Jonathan and the grandson of Saul. Saul the attempted murderer of David. Saul... the man who was constantly sinning against God and wouldn't even admit to his mistakes; instead, he blamed them on the people of Israel (1 Samuel 15:1-21). The man who, because he was so consumed by pride, ruined his relationships with others.

But Mephibosheth was nothing like Saul. He was not consumed and driven by jealousy, as was Saul. He was not prideful in the same aspect as Saul, but instead self-conscious to the point of thinking that he belonged in a city called Lo-debar (2 Samuel 9:5) — a city of "no production," as the name means.

I've said it once, and I'll say it again, your family tree does not disqualify you... or qualify you. We can't ride on our parent's relationship with God. We need a relationship with Him of our own. We can't ride on the coattails of a well-known last name.

You don't need a well-known last name, and having one doesn't automatically "qualify" us. You don't need to have served God for forty years. We just need to be willing. A simple truth that we don't like to acknowledge is that *no one* is qualified to do work for the Kingdom. We're all human. We all make mistakes. We're all sinners in need of a Savior.

We all fall short. We aren't perfect… but that's okay. God always uses imperfect people to bring about His perfect will. Amos, David, Gideon, Moses… and many more.

CHAPTER ELEVEN:
Support Systems

*"And though a man might prevail against one who is
alone, two will withstand him—*
a threefold cord is not quickly broken*."*
— Ecclesiastes 4:12 (ESV)

For most of my life, I was used to being alone. I found pride in being able to do all that I was doing without a family supporting me. When my parents kicked me out at 18, it became clear that I would not have the typical college experience.

Most college students have their parents to depend on. They get to experience independent living, but their parents act as a safety net if they get in over their heads. When I realized I was on my own for some of the most critical years of my life, I became obsessed with the idea of doing everything on my own.

I didn't need a family. I didn't need anyone. I got this far alone, so I thought I could go without anyone for the rest of my life. Independence was important… right? I needed to be able to do everything on my own… right?

My definition of independence was utterly wrong. I had convinced myself that I was just being independent when I was really trying to cope with the fact that no one was there for me by "never needing anyone." Independence *is* being able to do things on your own, but it's also not being afraid to ask for help when you need it. It's not an attitude of "I can do it all on my own."

"No man is an island to themselves entire of itself;
every man is a piece of the continent,
a part of the main."
-- John Donne

This quote is true spiritually and physically. Many studies show isolation can cause damaging effects. We need socialization to get through life. Eventually, a couple of people chipped away at my cold exterior. I only showed who I truly was to Harrison and left everyone out in the cold.

College brought me a support system that I never thought I could have. Friends who were like-minded and would give advice with ministry or Bible study. It was really iron sharpening iron (Proverbs 27:17)... something I never got to have outside of Harrison. I never had a good support system before then.

I was raised in a home that was physically and emotionally abusive. It set the standard for how I would allow people to treat me. What most people would consider toxic, I thought, "wasn't that bad." Because of this, I found myself getting into toxic relationships of many kinds without even realizing it. I would seek out people like my parents. I didn't even know I was doing this at the time, but I would surround myself with people who treated me the way I was used to.

People who were secretly happy when I would fail. Friends who would only ever talk to me or hang out with me when they needed me. Never would I get a response when I needed something. Unless they made plans, there were no plans.

I couldn't relate to people who were happy and mentally healthy. Their affection would make me feel awkward, as it wasn't something I was used to. Their compliments when I did something well would throw me off, as I was used to criticism...even if I had done it perfectly.

Their positivity was something that I couldn't understand; couldn't they see all of these bad things? Harrison was one of the first people like this that I became comfortable being around. But I was always waiting for his kind and honest demeanor to change. There was no way that he was really as good as he seemed — it had to be too good to be true for me.

In college, I started surrounding myself with people like Harrison and forming godly relationships that significantly changed my life. Our conversations would be really educational at times. They would hold me accountable when I started slacking or drifting. They would encourage me to read and pray... maybe even send me a verse of the day.

It's very important who we surround ourselves with. They can be very influential on us. The Bible is full of beautiful examples of GODLY friendships and romantic relationships. If you study them out, you can find common characteristics of a godly relationship (platonic and romantic). Don't allow yourself to be treated differently, and don't treat others that way.

With these new relationships (paired with my already existing relationship with Harrison), I realized things I was refusing to acknowledge about myself. I didn't like to acknowledge a lot, actually. I kept hiding my true emotions from everyone... including myself. I kept pushing everything down, thinking it would eventually disappear. I felt I had forgiven and moved on, but I really hadn't.

> *"In order to heal, you have to stop*
> *pretending it doesn't hurt."*

This phrase circled around social media for weeks. This phrase is a brutal truth we all must learn. The first step towards healing is acknowledging the hurt.

You have to be honest with both yourself and God. His love can't transform you while you're convinced it can't. It can't take effect if you believe it doesn't need to transform you. God won't force a work on you. You have to be receptive. I had to stop pretending I was okay because I was far from it. I wasn't okay, and it took having supportive friends and a supportive fiancé to feel comfortable admitting it out loud.

I also realized that I was wrong about myself. I was still clinging to the reason why I was treated the way I was. I still didn't know; I didn't learn about why until my junior year. I spent half of college still convinced that I was unlovable. I thought that Harrison and his family were just an anomaly. I thought that I was just some vessel for pain. Someone for people to take their anger and regrets out on. I felt that I didn't serve any other purpose.

But what I didn't realize (or want to acknowledge) was that I was really a vessel *for God*. Someone bought and chosen through the ultimate sacrifice of the cross. My purpose was to not be a punching bag but to help others being treated as punching bags. To show them that recovery is possible.

To show them that the pain won't last forever. To show them that there really is hope found in Jesus, that there is purpose to the pain. I was never a vessel for pain... I was a vessel for Him. My identity wasn't found in the hurt. It wasn't found in the abuse.

I wasn't a victim,
I was a victor -- through Him.
My identity was found in Him.
It always will be.

Hiding behind a mask of lies was much easier than confronting my raw feelings. I didn't have to look at the mess that was in my past. I could keep going forward, acting as if nothing was really wrong. Dressing up my brokenness and parading it around like it was anything else just distracted me from healing. I needed to stop pretending that it didn't hurt.

Ignoring the pain didn't make it go away. Filling my life with distractions didn't deafen the cry of my soul. At the end of the day... when I was all alone in my bed... the heaviness was still there. Sometimes it takes having those godly relationships in your life to point out what you are ignoring. Harrison has always been my biggest supporter, but he has always been honest with me.

Anytime I developed a mindset that wasn't healthy, he would be the first one to point it out. He was the first to call me out when I started talking about myself in ways that weren't conducive to my healing process. It doesn't have to be a romantic partner. It could be a friend. A counselor. A pastor. A youth leader. You don't have to face it all alone, no matter what your brain may tell you.

There are people who care for you more than you realize. Don't be afraid to reach out to them. There is no problem with asking for help. For so long, I was worried about being honest with the people around me because I thought they would start viewing me differently. I thought that they would look at me as someone weak because I had been through so much. What really happened was that they looked at me as someone who was strong because I had been through so much. I wasn't weak or pathetic in their eyes.

When we need help, the worst thing we can do is stay silent. I've been there. I've done that. It doesn't help. Talk to the people you trust about how you are truly feeling. There is nothing wrong with asking for help. I'm a fan of people who think they need to go to a therapist actually *going* to a therapist.

Half the battle is asking for help when you need it.

There is a massive stigma around seeking medical help for mental health right now. I just want to make it very clear --there is nothing wrong with being a Christian and still going to a therapist, counselor, or any other mental health professional. We have to recognize that, yes, God can and will "fix" me, and He might use the therapist to do it.

Going to a therapist can let you have a one-on-one conversation that can aid your attempt to make God your number one priority. While at a therapist or counselor, you can tell your darkest secrets to someone who *legally* can't tell someone else about it (within the guidelines of confidentiality).

If you've been burned by this before, and someone told other people everything that you trusted them with... a therapist might be an excellent option for you. Unless you disclose that you plan to hurt yourself or someone else, someone else is hurting you, or receiving a subpoena... it is *illegal* for them to tell others about what you open up to them about.

Think about it this way: Who do you go to when you are sick and need some medicine? A doctor. Does that mean that you don't have faith that God could heal you? Of course not! And does anyone question you when you tell them you are going to the doctor? No.

Why, then, is it any different for you to go to a therapist/counselor if you feel it would benefit your mental health? There's a stigma attached to getting treatment for mental health that is entirely wrong. If you're seeing a therapist (hey... *I'm* studying to be a therapist), that doesn't make you any less Christian.

Let's go back to the Bible. The story in 2 Kings 20:1-8 describes Hezekiah's illness being cured. God tells Hezekiah that

106

his illness will kill him, and Hezekiah begs to live. God directs Hezekiah to:

> *"Take a lump of figs.*
> *And they took and laid it on the boil,*
> *and he recovered."*
> *2 Kings 20:7 (KJV)*

The Benson commentary remarks on this story with some interesting points... *"Though the deliverance was certainly promised, yet means must be used, and those suitable. The figs would help to ripen the bile, and bring it to a head, that the matter of the disease might be discharged that way. This means, however, would have been altogether insufficient of itself to effect so sudden and complete a cure, without the co-operation of the divine power, to which the king's restoration to health is chiefly to be ascribed."*

Sometimes God uses simple remedies... like medicine, physical therapy, etc. ... to heal us. God used the figs in the process of healing Hezekiah. The figs were like a form of treatment. The figs would bring out all of the gross pus and bile. It would act as a disinfectant of sorts.

Community is vital in recovery. Having a support system can greatly help us in the midst of our recovery process. Sometimes God sends us people that serve to remind us that we are loved, heard, and seen. This can be by a close friend, significant other, and even a therapist.

It's important that someone trying to recover from trauma is surrounded by people who will support and encourage them. It can make a world of a difference.

Don't be afraid to ask for help when you need it.
Some people are willing to offer you their help in any way they can.

CHAPTER TWELVE:
The Start of Forgiveness

*"Let us hold fast the confession of our hope without wavering, **for He who promised is faithful.**"*
— Hebrews 10:23 (ESV)

"A grudge is a much heavier burden to carry than a cross."
— Author Unknown

By my junior year of college, I thought I had moved on. I felt like I had forgiven them all for any part they had played. I thought that it honestly did not bother me anymore. The nightmares came less. I could sleep at night peacefully for the first time in a decade. Everything seemed to be over. The storm seemed to finally be passing. I could move on and never think about the years that haunted me ever again.

I quickly realized that this was not the case. In my junior year, my mother (who had been having countless affairs up to this point) decided she wanted a divorce. You would think that this wouldn't bother me with a relationship as rocky and toxic as the one I had with my parents. At first, I thought that it didn't. *Good,* I thought when I heard the news. *Now I won't have to deal with either of them anymore. This is clearly an excellent time to cut ties.*

But the talk of divorce bothered me more than I realized. My mother filed an order of protection at the time after some coaxing from her friends. She went as far as adding the children into the order, preventing him from seeing any of them. My dad was separated from the children he loved and adored. I, who experienced so much pain at his hand, started to feel bad for him. While I acknowledge that my dad was very abusive toward me, my mother had no reason to file that order at the time. By this point, my dad spent nearly every hour of the day lying down on the couch... too ridden by health conditions to really move around. He wasn't physically capable of abusing anyone at this point... even if he wanted to.

To make matters worse, the divorce process started after a particularly bad episode that caused my dad to be put on a respirator. He was even described by his doctor as a vegetable. By all accounts, he should have died. But he didn't. I remember being relieved when I heard.

I was shocked...
then relieved...
then shocked that I was relieved.

Maybe I had truly forgiven him? Looking back now, this was the start of my long road to forgiveness. That instance of relief sparked the realization that I genuinely *could* forgive him. It *was* possible.

I convinced myself even more that I had moved on once I started to feel pity and even humanize my dad. When a social worker was working on my dad's discharge plan, she asked my mother if there was enough support in the home to take care of him. A cheerful no was given... resulting in him being placed in a nursing home.

Another person in my dad's life had failed him. This took me years to accept, but my dad's life was not much better than mine. He experienced much of what I did. He just couldn't break the cycle.

Before my dad was released, I visited him. Harrison and I brought him a present — some sweatpants, diabetic diet-approved trail mix, and a bag of jerky. Harrison held my hand as we entered the room... but my dad wasn't there.

We found him roaming the halls. He was in a wheelchair. He seemed so optimistic. He offered to financially support the missions (AYC) trip to Taiwan that Harrison and I planned to take before it was canceled due to COVID-19. I had never had an interaction with my dad like that before.

Looking back now, I wish I could have pushed past my pride and bitterness and attempted to have a relationship with him. I didn't. Even if he didn't reciprocate or accept my attempts, then… I would have been able to say I tried. My walls were still up and as tall as ever. I didn't trust this new dad.

> There had to be something sinister
> going on below the surface.

The visit went well. One thing I can take comfort in is that whenever I saw my dad, I tried to make him feel loved. I didn't refuse a hug. I said that I loved him. I told him I prayed for him whenever he complained about a symptom. I did try to at least make a connection when I could. I answered almost all the messages. I liked or responded to nearly all the comments. I realized during that time something that has stuck with me ever since…

> You will always regret acting on your bitterness,
> but you will never regret being the bigger person.

There will never be a situation where we regret treating someone the way we wish to be treated, but we will regret saying things that cut the other person to the core. Using phrases that we know make them feel diminished and unloved. We will never regret being a light to them, but we will regret being a hindrance. We need to get over our pride before it's too late.

* * *

My dad eventually moved back in with them, but things were never the same. My mom and my dad were officially separated. She ended up getting engaged twice within the next two years while they were still legally married and living together. It bothered me that they weren't together, but I didn't want to tell them it did.

Whatever they had seemed to work. They seemed to still care about each other in a platonic way. They lived together... and sometimes, my mom's fiancé moved in with them. Whatever it was... they made it work. But it bothered me. Deep down, my inner child was grieving. I just didn't know how to express that.

The thing is... though their marriage was flawed... I was always comforted by the fact that they were still together. At the end of the day, no matter what happened between us, they still had each other. They loved each other — they felt loved. Now they weren't together. I didn't think that it was fair to my dad. I didn't think I would ever like my mom's boyfriends or fiancés. They tended to be creepy or used her for free food and rent.

I started viewing my dad in a different light. I took time to humanize him. I was, not realizing it yet, starting to develop empathy for him. This stage in my life opened up the door to forgiveness.

In social work, there's an essential skill called *perspective taking*. It is precisely what it sounds like. It's where we take time to understand things from another person's point of view. This is a crucial step in developing empathy.

Sympathy and empathy are often viewed as the same thing, but they aren't. *Sympathy* is feeling bad for someone. This is what I was doing at first -- I felt terrible for my dad and his circumstances. *Empathy* is the ability to put yourself in someone else's shoes and understand their feelings. It involves a little bit of emotional intelligence.

When you feel bad for someone for what they are experiencing... it's sympathy; when you can relate to and understand what they're feeling.... It's empathy. Perspective-taking plays a massive role in the development of empathy.

I started developing empathy for my dad. I began to really think about how different experiences in his life affected his outcome. I hadn't fully forgiven him yet, but I was in the beginning stage of the process.

Process.

It's a word that's been stuck in my mind for years. It's a word that's been seared into my brain. The symphony of my life. It's all a process. I didn't wake up one day and forget everything that had happened to me or everything that they did to me. I didn't make a choice to forgive just once — it was a daily battle. I had to wake up every day and choose to forgive… choose to continue the process.

Some days I didn't have the strength to say yes. If I'm being honest, *most* days, I woke up struggling with choosing to continue in my path of forgiveness. But I didn't need to be strong.

"The Lord is their strength,
*and **He is the saving strength** of His anointed."*
Psalm 28:8 (KJV)

God became my saving strength. He was working on me. He was softening the heart that I hardened. The bitterness that I was harboring… that cold, calloused heart I had toward them… God took that out and gave me a new heart. A fleshly heart (Ezekiel 36:26). He can take out that heart hardened toward those that have hurt us and replace it with a soft heart — one ready to forgive and show mercy. The calluses I worked so hard to build up around it began to fall off my junior year of college.

Many people say that college is the most important time of your life. When most people say this, they're referencing all of the education you get or the social connections you make. This statement was true for me in different ways. God was preparing a way for me. He was doing a work that I never thought possible.

He was using what would have been a tragedy if my dad had died to show me that recovery is possible; forgiveness is possible. For everyone. Even me.

Forgiveness is possible. Even forgiveness for the people who treated you in ways you'll never feel comfortable expressing. Even after doing unspeakable things to you. This was just the start for me. This is just the start for you.

CHAPTER THIRTEEN:
It's Never too Late

*"Who is a God like you, **pardoning iniquity and passing over transgression** for the remnant of his inheritance? He does not retain his anger forever, **because he delights in steadfast love.**"*
— Micah 7:18 (ESV)

On June 18th of the year 2021, my dad passed away. We still don't really know why. They ended up faulting one of his many health complications. I was once again faced with not having a definite answer. I didn't live with my parents at this point. I lived in the house Harrison and I would live in when we got married. I was holding down the fort until December 18th came.

That day, I had to attend a birthday party for my roommate (a friend who was living with me for the summer). Her surprise party was at three o'clock that afternoon. Around twelve, my sister called me to tell me my dad was dead.

"Wait, what?" I said.
"You're joking, right?"

I couldn't believe it. I refused to believe it. We knew he would die earlier in life, but we expected it to be in his 50s or 60s. What we didn't expect was for him to pass away at 45. My life as I knew it came crashing down in those four words… "Kimi, Dad is dead."

At first, I thought I would be fine. After all, this is my abusive father we're talking about. I figured I would be a little sad about it, but then I assumed I would quickly move on. It took me until the next day to realize what that really meant. The reality hadn't quite set in yet.

It was the second time I had to grieve the loss of my father. When I was younger, I grieved the loss of his support, presence, and availability in my life. This time, I had to actually grieve him being gone. Forever. And there was nothing I could do to change that.

I would never have the chance to develop the relationship I thought we would eventually have. I thought that eventually, they would all get over their bias against me, and we would be a real family. A hope I held since I was young.

On that day...
that hope died with him.

God has a funny way of using circumstances we view as unusable. When I heard about my dad's death, I was partially relieved. He would never be able to hurt me again. I would never be disappointed by him again. But in the wake of my broken dreams, I found restoration.

I didn't sit with my thoughts for long because the party was starting at three o'clock, and we needed to leave a little early to ensure we got there before she did. I knew that she would have completely understood had I not shown up, but at the same time... I have never really been the person to consider my own feelings and needs above others. As I have mentioned, being raised by people with narcissistic tendencies... I was trained to be that way. I couldn't shut it off... even on a day like this. I acted like everything was okay and even smiled for a few pictures. No one knew a thing.

After we left the party, Harrison took me out for retail therapy. I tend to cope in unhealthy ways, and going to every thrift, discount, and bargain store I can find is one of them. But he knew I loved shopping. He knew that deciding how much I spent and what I spent it on helped me feel like I had some form of control. During stressful times when I feel like everything is spiraling out of control, I need a reminder that I do get to control some things in my life. He knew I needed to channel my emotions on something. To feel something. He knew I needed this.

While strolling through the stationary aisle, I saw a small notebook that said "wait, what?' on the front. I was floored. That was exactly what I said when I heard the news. I picked it up and turned it around in my hands. It was $2.00, and I debated buying it. I've always used writing to cope.

It was the healthiest coping mechanism I had.

I put it in Harrison's hands before I could change my mind. He didn't say a word and grabbed my hand as we walked out of the aisle I always spend too much money in. I felt stupid buying it, but Harrison didn't let me put it back. I think he could tell I bought it for a reason. I just didn't want to admit it out loud.

I didn't want to call it my "grief journal" because, at the time, it didn't feel like I had anything to grieve over. I didn't name it anything, but I decided to journal in it every day until I ran out of pages. I would make an entry pouring out all my feelings onto the small pages and copy down a verse from the Bible that was inspiring or a reminder I needed that day. If you're feeling any form of grief while reading this, I highly suggest starting one of your own.

Some of the entries I would title "Dear God," and others I would just immediately start writing in. Writing out what I felt without worrying about anyone else reading and making judgments about me was so freeing. I poured out my unfiltered thoughts without stopping to make them sound eloquent, so I could use them later. It was a raw expression of my state of being.

It's an interesting thing to look through. You can see my progress through my own words. My first entry went like this:

Dear God,
Dad died in his sleep early this morning. They thought that he was just sleeping in and didn't realize until lunch that something was wrong. They said his lips were pale, and his face was already turning purple. I'm starting a "grief journal" to let out all of my emotions (or lack of emotion) without fear of judgment. I don't know how to feel right now. This was something that I had wanted for a long time when I was younger. I thought that if my dad died, all my problems would disappear. I was tired of suffering at his hands. I feel guilty for feeling that for so long. I feel guilty for not feeling sad. I don't know how I feel. I'm a little sad. I'm very

confused. I think I'm still in shock. I'm not sure what the proper response is when your abusive father dies. I guess there is no blueprint for that. I feel weird knowing I'll never see him again, but in the same token, I was always so scared when he was around. I don't know how to feel. I don't really feel anything at all. That can't be normal. I'm a social worker. Shouldn't I be trained to handle this? I only cried once today when Harrison's dad was trying to give me support. It was like he assured me that it was okay to not feel okay. Like I didn't have to have it all together. I don't know. I'm rambling. I don't know what I'm feeling. It doesn't seem like I'm feeling anything at all. I'm numb.

I was completely confused about what to feel. I felt guilty for how I felt in many ways. I was significantly impacted by his death... more than I thought I would have been. For some reason, that felt wrong. I felt like an imposter. I didn't have a stable relationship with him... so I didn't have a reason to be sad.

So many people lose their dad, and they're devastated because they were so close to their father. To me, I felt like I didn't deserve to be sad... like expressing my sorrow would invalidate the feelings of those who lost a dad who was close to them. I felt like a hypocrite.

To me, I felt like my feelings were invalid.
Hypocritical.
Unreasonable.

I felt like being sad that my dad died made me a hypocrite. But then I realized that it made me a Christian -- "Christ-like." To love others even if they don't love us back; that's being Christ-like.

*"But I say to you, **love your enemies,** bless those who curse you, do good to **those who hate you,** and **pray for those who spitefully use you** and persecute you."*
Matthew 5:44 (NKJV)

The next day was the memorial service for Harrison's great aunt. Once again... I did the thing I always did; I stuffed my emotions deep down inside and went into the supportive role I was so used to filling. I have always used this trait to avoid confronting my feelings. If I was always worried about other people, I could act like my feelings didn't exist.

But I had them.
I needed to work through them.

It was such a weird feeling... going to something that I knew I would be arranging soon. Being around people who were grieving and trying to be supportive... but having a fresh wound myself. At this point, I still didn't know how or what I should feel.

After the service, Harrison and I made our way to my parents' house. It would be the first time going back since Thanksgiving when we dropped off food for them to have a good Thanksgiving meal. But this time, he wouldn't be there. I was full of dread.

I felt empty walking in. Empty talking to them. Empty trying to appear fine when we all knew things would never be the same again. Most of my family has always coped with stress by running from responsibilities. The brunt of the conversation on what to do next lay on Harrison and me. Not soon after we walked through the door, we were placed with the sole responsibility of deciding if we would have a funeral or cremate and hold a memorial service later.

That day, I realized I had hit the jackpot in finding a significant other. Harrison, who said he was determined to not let the responsibility fall onto me as it always has with my family, said he would handle things. I didn't express any of my feelings, but he was still able to sense them and make a plan for them.

I have always been the responsible one in my family. I would be the caretaker for my youngest sister, who has an intellectual disability, and my other sister, who is on the spectrum. I would solve my younger sister's school and relationship problems. I would change diapers when one of my younger sisters still wore them. I would talk to her when she wanted attention. I would buy both of them toys with the little money I had because I loved to see their faces light up when they got them.

When my parents got themselves in financial trouble, I would always be the one to help solve it. I would go grocery shopping with my mother to keep her on budget. I was the one they stole money from when they ran out, and I never made a big deal about it to them. I accepted that as part of my reality.

I had done so much to keep my family above the water while I was always the one drowning underneath. I allowed myself to become the glue that held them all together. But I was tired. I didn't think I had it in me to do it one last time. Harrison could tell and stepped into the role I usually played.

He made the important phone calls. He helped me write the obituary. His family handled the food and decor. We, together, made all of the decisions about the song selection and order of the service. Not because we wanted to be in control, but because we were offered no help. It was all up to me... as it usually was. Responsible Kimi had to do all the work. But this time, Responsible Kimi had a person she could lean on. Someone who would help bear the load.

It may be a little "beside the point," but I also learned in this process that it truly does matter who you marry. You need someone you can depend on to hold you up when you feel like falling apart. Someone you can count on when things get tough. But also someone who will laugh with you during the high points. Someone who will be your support regardless of the circumstances.

While we were visiting at my parents' house, my mother brought out something I forgot I always wanted. When I was very young, and my dad was still preaching, he had a Thompson-Chain reference Bible. I always envied it. It was black leather with gold trim on the outside of the pages. It contained commentary notes at the bottom and references down the middle. My mother handed it to me and told me that my dad would want me to have it. I then realized that no matter what he thought of me, he secretly respected my commitment to God.

While he was in church, he took notes over every sermon. While looking through a binder containing all these notes, Harrison joked that I got my intense note-taking from my dad.

This statement threw me for a loop. I have always instantly been willing to attribute my negative traits to my dad. I was always more than willing to blame him for things that went wrong in my life. When Harrison attributed this positive trait from him... I was offended at first.

I learned... yet another... lesson that day about my grieving and healing process. It's okay to talk about the bad but still acknowledge the good. Having good times with someone who has hurt you doesn't invalidate the bad that happened. What you experienced is still very real.

At the same time, don't let the bad invalidate the good. There's a *cognitive distortion* (an irrational and faulty way of perceiving things) called "disqualifying the positive." This cognitive distortion occurs when we dwell on the negative so much that it negates the positive. It happens when we get so fixated on the negative that we forget that there was something good. As the name states, we disqualify anything positive about the situation or experience. I was doing this a lot in my life.

I was so focused on the negative that I denied the existence of the positive. At the same time, I didn't want to acknowledge the positive; I was worried it would disqualify the negative. In simple terms, I was so worried about admitting that there were good experiences with my dad or that I inherited good traits from my dad because I feared no one would believe all the bad things I experienced.

I also struggled intensely with black and white thinking; this is another cognitive distortion where something has to be all one thing or all another thing (all good or all bad, for example). I believed wholeheartedly that if I chose to continue loving someone who hurt me, I couldn't set boundaries with them. I believed that I couldn't truly empathize with them while also acknowledging the hurt that they caused me. I thought that it had too be all of one thing or another, but never a mix of the two.

Throughout the next few years after my dad's death, I was learning that it is okay for things to have multiple layers. Things can be both good and bad. The bad doesn't take away from the good, and the good doesn't take away from the bad.

Before I started working to correct these distortions in my thinking, I was worried that people would question or deny my trauma if I admitted that there were a few happy moments amid the tragic moments.

You can fondly remember the good
and still acknowledge the bad.

It doesn't have to be all good or all bad.
It can be both.

It's okay to admit if it was both for you.

Looking through these pages of notes changed my outlook on my dad. It changed Harrison's opinion too. It made us realize something else. My dad was never this monster that we both despised. He was a living, breathing person *with a soul.* He experienced heartache that made him into the person he was. He was hurt. He felt pain. Pain that was just as real as mine.

As I mentioned, before he died, we recognized him as someone who deserved love… we just weren't ready to be the ones who would give it to him yet. On Thanksgiving of 2020, we took food over to their house. My sister later texted me that my parents were talking badly about the food… "you can tell that it's from Kimi." I was ready to have a mental breakdown. Even in trying to treat them like nothing ever happened, I was still the enemy. I didn't even cook the food, and it was still my fault they didn't like it.

At this point, the pain they caused me was irreconcilable.
I was done.
I didn't know what to do to fix the relationship.
Everything I did backfired.
Nothing was good enough for them.
I wasn't good enough for him.

Shortly after that Thanksgiving (before he passed away), my mother showed up at the place I was staying and tried to rope me into solving a problem she had gotten herself into again. I was living with Harrison's grandmother at that time. Harrison's grandmother answered the door and called for me in a voice that worried me.

I made my mother stay outside and explained that they could not stay with us. Harrison's grandmother did not need the paranoia that my parents would randomly show up at her house. She did not need to worry about someone coming to hurt us. My mother had no right to try to dump all of her "problems" off on me.

Harrison came to his grandmother's house ready to defend us if things went wrong. My mother and her fiancé (yes, my timeline is correct; she was with her fiance and not my dad...) were gone before he arrived. What he walked into was me sobbing on the couch inconsolably. I thought I had ruined everything. Granny wouldn't feel safe in her own home all because of me.

I ruined everything.
Just like *I* always did.

Harrison decided then that we needed to pray. This was the day we realized that my dad deserved love. This is also the day I started to believe that I was not responsible for the actions of my parents. Harrison wouldn't leave until I could admit it was not my fault. I did not ask her to come here. I did not give them the okay to come over here.

This short prayer meeting changed how we viewed them all. We both shook off some bitterness that we had been holding against them. The work that God did in us that day continued. But the day we saw the notes and the Bible... it multiplied. It gave us a weird sense of closure.

It opened the door for me to realize that I was not responsible for the actions of others. I never was. My childhood conditioned me to think it was always up to me to fix the consequences of others' actions.

This helped me realize that while I wasn't responsible for the actions of others...
I was responsible for how I *responded* to those actions.

After leaving my parents' house, Harrison and I decided to go to Olive Garden because we had a $40 gift card and figured it would be a good time to use it... given the circumstances. I wonder what the people who sat across from us thought of us. While there, we had a very deep and intense conversation about my dad. We concluded that my dad was a little like Paul... a sentence I never thought I would say.

*"For I do not understand my own actions. For I do not do what I want, **but I do the very thing that I hate.**"*
Romans 7:15 (ESV)

We realized that this was probably how my dad felt. He grew up being taught to express his emotions through violence. Someone he looked up to was forced out of his life when they went to prison for ten years. His mom struggled to raise him on her own. Her boyfriends would treat him horribly in secret.

My dad became the very thing that he hated. He didn't want to do what he was doing, but that was all he knew. He was no longer allowed to work... something he found his identity and had a sense of pride in. His wife walked out on their marriage many times, potentially leading to him not being the real father to one of my other siblings and me. His life was falling apart, and he resorted to the only way he knew to express his feelings.

He wanted to be good, but he felt he had done too much to return to God. He wanted to be like he was in church, but he felt he had gone too far to be used in ministry again. This is something that reconciled with him towards the end of his life. A couple of weeks before his death, he posted, "It is time for me to be about my Father's business." Harrison and I believe that he was in the process of turning his life around during the time he passed.

Remember:

You haven't gone too far that God's love can't run to you.

You haven't done so much that His love can't radically change your life. There is always hope. The Bible has example after example of people becoming new after encountering Jesus. People were healed. Sins were forgiven. Long-standing generational curses were stopped in their tracks. All it takes is *one encounter* with the miraculous Savior.

*"Therefore if anyone is in Christ, he is a new creation. **old things have passed away; behold, all things are become new.**" 2 Corinthians 5:17 (KJV)*

Once your past is under the blood, it is like it doesn't even exist anymore. The old has passed away — you've become new. Don't live your life believing that you've gone too far. His mercy extends beyond our recognition. His grace overtakes even the darkest of nights.

You can be new.
And it's never too late to be free from
the shame you carry with you.
There is no expiration date for healing.

CHAPTER FOURTEEN:
The Truth and Lies About
FORGIVENESS

*"bearing with one another, **and forgiving one another**, if anyone has a complaint against another; even as Christ forgave you, so you also must do."*
— *Colossians 3:13 (NKJV)*

A big part of my story is forgiving what I once thought was unforgivable. It makes sense that a large section of this book would be about forgiveness.

For the following few chapters, I will walk you through a few misconceptions I had concerning forgiveness. I will debunk them and show you that... while it may make sense at the time... these misconceptions are not actually logical. On the third day of my journal, you can see the remarkable difference God made in my time of grief:

Today is Father's Day. Of all days. After talking with Harrison, my family, and reading some of my dad's sermon notes... I don't feel so angry anymore. I was so bitter for so long. Now, I feel love. Harrison explained it best; before he died, I had humanized my dad. I could admit that, at the core, he was human. He had a soul. I could admit that because he was human and had a soul; he deserved love. Now, we (Harrison and I) both feel love toward him. It's a feeling I thought I would never have. My only regret is that I didn't get here sooner... before he died. I wish I had swallowed my pride and pushed past my bitterness. I just pray that he didn't die feeling alone. And I feel guilty for never being able to honestly show it. Don't get me wrong. I gave hugs, and I said, "I love you." I showed him support in my mother's string of affairs and the impending divorce. I didn't really feel the love that I was trying to show. I just wish I could have assured him that I forgave him in time. Because I did. I forgave him that Thanksgiving before he died after a prayer session with Harrison. In fact, both Harrison and I had forgiven him. I just hope he knew or could at least tell that I was choosing to forgive.

During this time, I realized what forgiveness really was. It wasn't just accepting an apology and moving on — I never got one. My first misconception of forgiveness was that forgiveness was just a one-time decision that I never had to think about again; forgiveness is a conscious decision that I have to continue making each day. When I would rise in the morning, I would be faced with the decision: be bitter or be forgiving?

It's also not easy. I made a lot of progress in my journey of healing. I had forgiven something I thought I would never be capable of forgiving. However, it was still a decision that I needed to make each day. Some days are hard. Some days I wake up from a nightmare about something he did to me, and I feel like I have to forgive all over again. But every day I decide to continue in forgiveness… it gets a little bit easier. I still have so much more to go, but I have come so far from where I started.

Forgiveness is a daily choice.

My second misconception was that it wasn't as big of a deal as people made it out to be. Sure, I had a lot to forgive. I had unspeakable things to forgive. But I (ignorantly) thought that since everyone else seemed to do it so easily, then it should be a walk in the park for me.

The reality is that forgiveness is hard. Moving on from trauma is hard. But it's possible. Now that you've read my testimony, you know I didn't have the best upbringing. But there is much that I haven't even typed out. There's so much you haven't read.

For a short summary — if you're just jumping into this chapter because of the title — I have experienced many heartbreaking experiences in my twenty-two years of living. Abuse. Neglect. Feeling like I'm not capable of being loved. People walking out of my life. Being dumped (multiple times). Seeking joy in things that could only bring sparks of fleeting happiness. Feeling miserable and depressed. Dealing with anxiety every single day. Experiencing symptoms of Complex Post-traumatic Stress Disorder (CPTSD) when I did finally get out. I could go on and on.

> Forgiving those who treated me in ways that (negatively) impacted me for the rest of my life... It saved me.

Another misconception I had was that forgiveness was only helpful for the person who was being forgiven. It was the "right thing to do," but it was also for my own sake. The thing I've learned about all of this is that the longer I went, harboring a grudge and unforgiveness in my heart, the more miserable I felt. It became a cage. And I willingly locked myself in it. I couldn't fully live my life that way.

Refusal to forgive only leads to a road of bitterness. A lust for revenge will only ever hold you captive. I couldn't move on without forgiveness. I realized that if I didn't forgive, I would remain shackled by the trauma I had experienced. A refusal to move on only stunts our emotional, mental, and spiritual growth. I couldn't live in freedom while willingly being shackled by the chains of unforgiveness.

> I had to realize that forgiveness wasn't a requirement... it was a *gift*.

I'm not going to make my story feel like a walk in the park — it was really hard for me to forgive the people who did those things to me. Multiple times, I thought I had forgiven them... but I really hadn't. I would throw myself on an altar with tears falling down my face. I was determined not to leave until I felt changed, but I also refused to expose all of my broken pieces to God.

I wanted to be healed... but on my own terms — just like Naaman (2 Kings 5 -- see Chapter Seven of this book for his full story). When I finally decided to let go and move on, I felt a huge weight lifted off my shoulders. I was no longer trapped in that cage.

No longer held hostage by my past.

By the grace of God, I have gotten to a place in my life where it doesn't matter if I ever get an apology. I don't need one anymore. God helped me forgive without them ever showing an ounce of regret or remorse. And I finally started living free. I was no longer holding on to all of that baggage -- the trauma of my family I had taken on, the trauma my family caused me, the pain, the bitterness -- that was never my place to carry around.

Their voices stopped lingering around as much. I could do things without immediately hearing their belittling. I was no longer waiting and daydreaming about the apology I would never receive.

Jesus had an interesting talk with Peter about forgiveness.

"Then came Peter to him, and said, 'Lord, how often shall my brother sin against me, and I forgive him? Up to seven times?'
Jesus said unto him, 'I do not say to you, up to seven times, but up to seventy times seven.'"
Matthew 18:21-22 (KJV)

Jesus wasn't saying that the limit of forgiving people was 77 or 490 times. Jesus showed us that we should forgive just as God has forgiven us — without a limitation. He even almost says that word for word in Matthew 6:14-15:

*"**For if you forgive men their trespasses, your Heavenly Father will also forgive you**. But if you do not forgive men their trespasses, neither will your Father forgive your trespasses."*
Matthew 6:14-15 (NKJV)

We have sinned against God countless times, and He still forgives us. Through him, we can forgive. No matter how big the betrayal. No matter how many occurrences. No matter if we never get an "I'm sorry."

In fact, we need to be able to get to a place where we are no longer looking for a limit on how often we should forgive. We don't need to ask for the cutoff when it's become "too much" to forgive. That's not how the model of forgiveness – God's perfect forgiveness – works. He has no limit. Neither should we. We need to stop looking for a limit and work towards being able to forgive without a limit.

To debunk another misconception I had about forgiveness: forgiveness isn't weak; it's empowering. We need to forgive others just like God has forgiven us.

"Be kind one to another, tenderhearted, forgiving one another, as God in Christ forgave you."
Ephesians 4:32 (NKJV)

"Bearing with one another and, if one has a complaint against another, forgiving each other; as the Lord has forgiven you, so you also must forgive."
Colossians 3:13 (ESV)

I could go on. Not only is forgiveness good for your soul, but it's also biblical. We have been forgiven of so much — we should forgive others in the same manner.

A few years ago, I was plagued with the phrase "forgive them anyway." It followed me everywhere — it popped up on my timeline in each social media app, people would often say it to me or around me, and it was a recurrent phrase during my quiet time with God.

But yet each time I heard it... I would roll my eyes internally. *Is someone who doesn't understand what I went through in my life and probably has never experienced anything "actually traumatic" going to tell **me** to just forgive people who have abused me my entire life...* was all I would think.

My self-righteous thoughts were another misconception about forgiveness. It doesn't take forgiving something like abuse to learn what forgiveness really is. Just because other people didn't have to forgive things "as deep" (the way I deemed it at the time) as I had to didn't mean that they didn't know what they were talking about.

It was true; some of the people who would preach to me that I should "just forgive, forget, and move on" were people who had never experienced abuse. They didn't understand the hold that trauma can have over someone. People speaking on something they didn't understand (as I viewed it) and minimizing the effects of abuse further pushed me to reject the message of forgiveness.

It made me want to hold onto the resentment and unforgiveness I had; I never thought that I would come to agree with their statement. This was all rooted in pride and self-righteousness, of course.

I began "gatekeeping" (or, in other words trying to determine who actually got a say when talking about) forgiveness in my mind. I thought that because they didn't experience something "as traumatic as me" (there's that self-righteous attitude rearing its ugly head again), they didn't have the right to try to teach me about forgiveness. The reality was that they did know what they were talking about... most of them at least.

In social work (or any counseling field, really), self-disclosure is a powerful tool. It helps establish ethos (your credibility) with your client. Too much self-disclosure shifts the focus on you, but a perfect amount can help the client trust your judgment. They can trust your judgment because you have been there before and/or you have knowledge of the subject. I feel it is also essential to establish it in this book.

After those life lessons I mentioned earlier, this has become the most prominent message I try to preach. I am not someone who is speaking on a topic with no prior experience or knowledge. I know all too well what holding on to unforgiveness can do. I also understand how hard it can be to forgive people who have caused so much pain in your life.

I say this so that you won't zone me out as I had done to so many people before. But you also have to recognize that people can understand things they didn't experience. Most of the time, they are speaking out of love, not correction or judgment.

They may not completely understand the pain, but they can recognize it. I can understand the pain. I understand the frustration.

But eventually, we must start living beyond the hurt. We must live beyond the brokenness... and forgiveness is a significant step in that process.

I'm going to be very transparent in this chapter: it's not easy to forgive people who have deeply hurt you. It often can seem impossible. But as hard as it can sometimes be, it is not *actually* impossible. I've been in that place where I did not think I could ever forgive certain people in my life. I had held on so tightly to the pain that they caused me that I couldn't view them as anything but monsters. Their actions had completely dehumanized them to me. Through this lens, I forgot that... at the end of the day... they were just broken and hurting people too. But the sympathy, empathy, and love I have for them now were lacking in all areas of my life then.

All I could think about was the anger displaced onto me. Me -- being so young that I can barely remember it -- taking up their slack and caring for kids I wasn't supposed to be responsible for. Me -- experiencing this the entire time I was with them -- being abused in almost every single category. If you can think of it, I have probably been hit with it or called it.

All I could think about were nights spent sleeping in my closet; sometimes I did this voluntarily to feel safe and other times (mostly during the day) against my will — I've had a love-hate relationship with small, dark spaces most of my life. Every time I saw their faces, I could only think about being that small, scared child. I would revert back to being a teenager so exhausted from trying to put up a fight and ultimately accepting defeat.

And if we're being honest here...
sometimes I still do.

I couldn't move on. I did not have the power within me to forgive those people who had caused me so much hurt for so many years. I didn't have the strength. Or the courage. I was holding on to tragedies and unwilling to release them... But God.

Sometimes we don't have it within us to forgive. Sometimes the hurt seems so overwhelming that we can't move, much less *move on*. But that's okay. We were never meant to rely on our own strength but instead on His. He will give us strength. We can depend on the community around us. Asking for help isn't a sign of weakness… it is a strength.

So how do we remain civil to people who have hurt us deeply? Remain calm and stop being so defensive. Think about it this way, if someone is determined and refuses to accept the truth about the situation, there's no point in wasting time trying to defend ourselves. They won't change their mind… no matter how masterfully crafted our defense is.

Remain cool, calm, and collected. Take a few moments to think before you act or speak anytime you have to interact with them. Pray for wisdom to do what is right. Pray for patience, so you don't slip into doing something wrong and/or hurtful. Don't allow your witness to suffer because you stooped down to their level.

His grace can be extended through us. When I don't feel I can forgive, I can recognize that through Him, I can. On those days where we fall short… maybe it's a little hard to be civil… maybe the reminders are too strong… on those days, His grace covers us. We can extend that grace that we have been shown.

I attended a church service once where a speaker talked about their journey with forgiveness. It was very convicting. I could feel how red my ears were getting… something that happens when I am nervous. I knew that forgiveness was something I needed to accept.

I had another Hannah-like (1 Samuel 1:13) prayer experience. I laid everything out. I cried. I pleaded. I did such a convincing job of "giving up my pain to God" that I even fooled myself.

While I thought I had truly poured out all of the resentment, anger, jealousy, and bitterness… there was still a tiny compartment in my heart left unopened. I didn't expose as much as I convinced myself that I did. Sometimes you don't realize how bad it is until it presents itself, and you realize that you've been nurturing its growth this whole time.

I had that altar experience during a service about forgiveness and never thought about it since. I harbored so much resentment and anger in my heart without even realizing it. I had thought that I had forgiven them. I had forgiven them then... or at least I *thought* I did... so why keep dwelling on it? At the time, I didn't realize that the altar experience was the start of my journey to forgiveness — *it was not a one-time and done type of thing.*

The neglect of continuing that prayer every day and intentionally working on forgiveness gave root to resentment. Feelings that I had not processed were building up underneath. Resentments that I did not work through were boiling below the surface... but I thought I was fine.

After all, I did have that one altar experience.

It took being locked inside the house for months at a time due to a global pandemic for me to actually process what happened to me and how to move on from it. That included revisiting the topic of forgiveness... the dreaded topic I always avoided.

I quickly realized that I did not "forgive and forget" in that singular instance as I had convinced myself all those years ago. It was much easier to let myself believe that I had moved on than to actually take the time to process and forgive.

As I've mentioned before, doing this meant I had to relive all those experiences I was trying to forget. It was much easier to accept that one altar experience as a change in my attitude towards them. If I allowed myself to believe that, I would not have to do any more work on changing my mindset. I did not have to spend any more time dwelling on it. I didn't have to spend any more time being transparent to God about it. I didn't have to open up about my real, raw feelings.

I chose the route that led to unforgiveness and resentment.

Another big misconception I had about forgiveness was that when I forgave someone, our relationship had to go back to the way it originally was. I thought that in order to truly forgive... I needed to put myself back into situations that were dangerous for me. The truth is that we don't have to put ourselves back into toxic relationships; when we forgive, we get to redesign these relationships.

Sometimes it is healthiest for us to love from a distance. You can completely forgive someone but still have space between you. You should never force yourself back into destructive environments because you feel that will signify that you have forgiven someone.

One day I was scrolling through Instagram when I saw a quote that made me realize this. For so long, I felt like an imposter. If I had genuinely forgive my parents... wouldn't I be living with them? Wouldn't I trust them again? Wouldn't things go back to our original normal?

"I believe in forgiveness with all my heart, but that does not mean repeatedly going back to entertain toxic relationships that are a threat to your mental health and well-being. Sometimes you not only need to forgive but also... move on."
— *Victor Jackson*

Sometimes it's best to love... from a distance.
Forgive... from a distance.
Show mercy... from a distance.
Give support... from a distance.

While I didn't move back in with them and place myself into dangerous situations... I *had* forgiven them. I didn't resent them anymore. I didn't harbor hatred for them in my heart anymore. Not one of them.

And the thing about that is that I could *never* have forgiven those people in my life on my own. I convinced myself that a few minutes of just going through the motions with no absolute surrender could lead to forgiveness.

As I've said, I don't hold power within myself to do that. I wasn't strong enough. I wasn't merciful enough. But I serve a God who does have that power. Through Him, I can forgive them. Truly. Completely. But it is crucial to fully surrender that pain we're holding on to. Don't be like me. Give it over to Him. He can help us forgive without an apology or even a sign of remorse from those who hurt us.

When I finally decided to relinquish control, I felt a huge weight lifted off my shoulders. I'm at a place in my life where it doesn't matter if I ever get an apology. Not from a place of resentment, but because I truly feel like I don't need one anymore.

After I realized that is when I finally started living free. I was no longer holding on to all of that baggage that I never had to carry around. I was no longer waiting and daydreaming about the apology I would never receive. Their voices stopped lingering around as much. I could do things without immediately hearing their belittling. Forgiveness isn't weak; it's empowering.

We need to forgive others just like God has forgiven us.

CHAPTER FIFTEEN:
The Biblical Basis of
Forgiveness

*"But they cried out with a loud voice and stopped their ears and rushed together… **And as they were stoning Stephen**, he called out, 'Lord Jesus, receive my spirit.' And falling to his knees he cried out with a loud voice, '**Lord, do not hold this sin against them**.' And when he had said this, he fell asleep."*
— *Acts 7:57-60 (ESV)*

During one of the rides home from my parents' house during the following weeks after my dad died, Harrison and I had another discussion about how we were feeling. As I said, at first, I didn't think that I had anything to grieve over. In reality, I had so much to grieve over. The loss of a father. The loss of a potential relationship. The loss of a hope. The loss of a constant for my mother.

There was a loss. I moved on from being angry and bitter at him too late. My one wish is that I could have pushed past myself and reached this reconciliation sooner. I wish I would have allowed God to do the work in me. But the best feeling… what I didn't regret… was no longer being bound in bitterness.

I no longer felt that weight that held me back. I felt free to tell my story in a way that wasn't harping on how bad he was. Humanizing the people who inflicted so much pain on me made me realize they were just lashing out against me due to all the pain they pent up. The stress. The betrayal *that they experienced* at the hand of the people they trusted most.

It wasn't personal. It wasn't some calculated attack on me. They were angry. They were hurting. They responded in the only way that they both knew how — screaming, getting physical, or severe punishment. They learned it from their parents as well.

If you feel like the next step in your recovery is forgiveness

— true forgiveness — start by trying to humanize them.

I know it feels better to view them as monsters without a soul. It feels better to not even think about them at all... to push everything down and numb yourself to it all. But you can't start processing pain that you pretend doesn't exist. You can't offer up your trauma to God if you refuse to believe or acknowledge that you have any.
It may feel impossible. How can God heal me from something *"this messed up?"* How can God make a way for me when *I* don't even see a way out?

Many churches have testimony nights for the purpose of building faith among the congregation. The purpose is that the testimony of one person will inspire another person. *If He did it for Suzy, surely He can do it for me.* The faith of one person can inspire confidence in others. This is why I'm writing this book. God has delivered me from everything written in this book and things that might never be printed on a page.

Situation after situation, He reminded me of why He is called Jehovah-Jireh (Genesis 22:8-14) -- my provider. He would provide for everything I needed. Groceries would be dropped off at the door when I thought I would starve over the summer. People from church would "feel like God was telling them" to give me five dollars so I could buy some snacks on days I hadn't eaten anything. They would "feel the nudge" to pray for me when I needed it most. They bought me new clothes for school every year. Christmas presents showed up on my doorstep each Christmas I had no gifts.

He reminded me of why He is called Jehovah-Shalom (Judges 6:24) -- my peacemaker. He calmed all of the raging waves in my heart and mind. He took me out of chaos and gave me a peaceful place to stay. He reminds me... to this day... that rest is good for me. Jehovah-Shalom... He gives me peace. He can do the same for you.

He reminded me of why He is called Jehovah-Shammah (Ezra 48:35) -- my constant. His presence never left me. Even when I tried to run from Him. Even when I tried to hide from Him. He was ever-present during my darkest hours. He never left my side. My support when I had no other. I didn't have to face one heartbreak on my own.

The season of processing my dad's death... I discovered why He is called Jehovah-Rapha (Exodus 15:26). It made me realize that God can heal much more than I thought possible. I knew that He could heal diseases... I had seen it before. I knew He could heal ailments in the mind... I had seen it before. I never thought about God healing and fixing *emotions* that I had toward someone. I didn't think about God being able to turn hatred and bitterness into love... until He did it for me.

I knew that He was able to do: *"**exceedingly abundantly** above all that we ask or think, according to the power that works in us."*
Ephesians 3:20 (NKJV)

But... remembering that during a never-ending storm is a whole different story. This may be something that you need to write on a post-it note and stick all around your bedroom or house... God can do the things you doubt He can do. It's hard to remember that when you're facing what seems like twenty-foot waves and your boat has a hole in it.

Think of Gideon. Being called a mighty warrior before he was one, Gideon found himself in the middle of a war. He needed an army and gathered people to serve in it. Judges 7 documents an interesting exchange between God and Gideon.

God told Gideon that he had too many men with him. He told Gideon to send those who were afraid home... twenty-two thousand left and ten thousand remained. Still, the Lord told him that he had too many men with him.

God told Gideon to take his men to get some water, and Gideon did so. While getting a drink of water, some men cupped water in their hands to drink the water like a dog would, and others kneeled down to get a drink (Judges 7:5-7). God told Gideon to send those who kneeled home, and Gideon did so.

Nine thousand and seven hundred men were sent home. Three hundred remained. An army of over twenty-two thousand went down to *three hundred men.*

It seemed impossible for God to deliver an entire nation with such a small army. Many people probably didn't think that God could do it. But He did. Go throughout the Bible, and you'll see countless people doubting God. But He proves Himself every time.

Maybe instead of questioning God, we should spend more time trying to build our faith. Perhaps we should spend time talking to others who have been through similar situations. Maybe we should read some Bible stories about humans... just like you and me... who were up against impossible odds but still won because they had the God of angel armies fighting for them.

God can do more than we can even *think* to ask. He *can* do exceedingly abundantly. He can give us the strength to forgive when we don't have it. He can lend us His love to extend to those we feel we could never love. Don't just take it from me.

Ask the ordinary human beings found all throughout the Bible who forgave. Ask Esau, who forgave Jacob (later Israel) for taking everything that was rightfully Esau's — the birthright and the blessing (Genesis 33). Ask Stephen... *who stood in front of the people ready to stone him...* and still asked God to forgive them before he died (Acts 7). Ask Joseph, who forgave his brothers for *selling him into slavery* and telling their father that he was dead (Genesis 50). And lastly, ask Paul.

"At my first answer no man stood with me, but all men forsook me: ***I pray God that it may not be laid to their charge.""*** *2 Timothy 4:16 (KJV)*

No man stood with me. All men forsook me. That sounds very familiar to me. I know the crushing feeling when you realize that, outside of God, you are all alone. That no other human is there, especially when you were the one pushing everyone away before they could get too close.

In Stephen's story of forgiveness, it doesn't show how the people who stoned him reacted. I'm sure they felt confused. Maybe a few of them felt a twinge of guilt that quickly disappeared. If someone, who was being stoned to death, could forgive those who murdered him... what makes us so dignified in our harboring bitterness and grudges?

Esau forgave Jacob for stealing his whole identity, basically. All Esau could be (back in those times) was heavily based on getting the birthright and blessing. Esau still forgave Jacob for stealing the life he could have had... yet I can't even handle people copying me.

Joseph... who just wanted acceptance (think about it... he was the weird "dreamer")... but was given nothing but rejection by his brothers. They told his dad that he was dead. They *sold* him into slavery like he meant *nothing* to them. But I can't forgive someone who forgets to invite me to an outing.

The problem with forgiveness is that we only want to give it when we feel they deserve it. We only want to forgive when we are given an apology — when someone comes crawling back and begging us to forgive them. They need to *deserve* it. That line of thinking oozes with pride.

Most of the great ideas Harrison and I come up with are through conversations with each other. During the car ride home, Harrison brought up the idea of being due something versus deserving something. Just because you're due, something doesn't necessarily mean you deserve something. Especially when God steps in.

Think of it this way... applied to the idea of forgiveness... we think those who treat us wrong don't *deserve* our forgiveness. We feel like we have ownership of their wrongdoing and now get to determine if they should be punished severely for it. We think they deserve this punishment, and we deserve revenge. True, they are *due* punishment for how they treated us... just like we're due punishment for the way we have treated other people.

Taking it a step further, we are due (*and* deserve) punishment for our sins... but God stepped in. He took all the punishment we were due (and deserved) and displaced it. He created a way for our sins to be taken care of... without us suffering that pain.

The people who treat us wrong aren't actually due our anger; they're actually due the love of God. They are due us extending the grace that was shown to us. They are due and deserve us to show the love that we were given. Our humanity... our flesh... does not agree. It wants to show that anger. It wants to dish out punishment and revenge.

The parable of the prodigal son appears in Luke 15:11-32. Long story short... a son decides that he would like his inheritance early... *before* his dad dies. After the son received the inheritance, he left town... he left the father, who graciously said yes and gave him the blessing. To summarize a bit of his story, he blows all of his inheritance and finds himself in a pig pen. When he finally comes to his senses, he returns to his father's house — only to find his dad running to him (something older men did *not* do at the time).

In the eyes of our flesh, the son was due his father putting him to work to pay off the money he lost. But the dad recognized that the son was really due to the extension of the love of God. He didn't *deserve* harsh punishment in his father's eyes.

Extending forgiveness is freeing for us, freeing for those we are forgiving, and freeing for anyone else impacted by the relationship strain. I know it seems complicated, but the great thing is that it's a process. Some days may feel like you're making more progress than others... and that's completely normal.

Don't stress over where you are compared to where someone else is. We're all on different journeys. We haven't all lived the same life. Progress looks different for each person.

Trust God.
Trust the process.
Trust God in the process.

CHAPTER SIXTEEN:
The Power of Unlearning

*"He who dwells in the shelter of the Most High **will abide in the shadow of the Almighty.** I will say to the Lord, 'My refuge and my fortress, my God, in whom I trust.'"*
— Psalm 91:1-2 (ESV)

I have never been able to sleep in a room without a light that I could turn on if I needed it. This can easily be traced back to a few experiences I had as a kid and... more recently... symptoms of CPTSD that I have been trying to deny. I have nightmares surrounding memories from my childhood. Some are recurring. Sometimes they are older memories I didn't realize I had. As a result, I *need* to have a light that I can turn on to remind myself that I am okay.

This became a problem when I lived alone right before Harrison and I married. The light in my room blew, I didn't have a very bright lamp, and it was a complicated light fixture (to me at least), so I had no idea how to take it apart to change the light bulb. Since we weren't married yet, Harrison couldn't come over and fix it... because we would be in the house alone. I also was never out of the house when he was available to fix it.

As a result, I spent a month or two sleeping on the couch in the living room. It made no sense to everyone because I love sleeping in absolute darkness... so why would I need a light? It came down to control... as most things do with me. I wanted to be able to control the light. I wanted to be able to turn it on after a nightmare. I needed the reassurance that only light could give when my heart was racing, and my thoughts were spiraling.

This was a dependency I unlearned when Harrison and I got married. The presence of another person helped calm me. It helped me to become less reliant on needing light. Something I thought would never be possible happened. I could sleep in a room even if there wasn't a light source. It was a massive step for me.

I had unlearned a response to trauma that wasn't exactly healthy. It forced me to spend months on a couch and gave me horrible back pain. This is a small example of one of the biggest lessons I learned about recovery.

When you experience a rough upbringing, you learn toxic behaviors and/or unhealthy coping mechanisms. There's no way around it. Even if you think you didn't, some will pop up later. Those behaviors will creep up on you without warning, and one day you will find yourself doing things that you saw others doing when you were a child. Things that you don't even pick up on in your day-to-day life.

We can become products of the environment that we live in or have lived in. We see the behaviors of those around us... we hear the words they're saying... and we start to model them. We don't always recognize this consciously. It may take deliberate reflection on *why* we act in a certain manner.

And more likely than not, we will trace it back to the words, mannerisms, and behaviors modeled in front of us for so many years. This is called **observational learning**. We see or hear something, and then we begin to copy it. And as we continue copying it, it becomes a habit that becomes a learned behavior. *Our* behaviors. *Our* words. *Our* mannerisms.

For me, I developed toxic behaviors as a way to cope with what was going on around me. At the time, I didn't recognize them as being unhealthy. I thought that I was doing the best I could to survive. In reality, these coping mechanisms would negatively impact my life in the long run. I would end up self-sabotaging many times.

I decided that the best course of action to protect myself was to never let anyone in. As mentioned earlier, I would build walls between myself and the outside world to cope with the fact that I was alone. I thought I couldn't get hurt if I never got close to another person. If I didn't have someone, they could never leave me.

The minute someone started getting too close to me and the truth about my life, I would cut them off. I would ignore them until they stopped trying to be friends with me. I wouldn't respond to texts. I ignored calls. I bailed on plans.

I thought that this was a justified response. I was unlovable, remember? The closer they got to me, the closer they would get to see what my family saw. If I wasn't enough for them... I wasn't enough for anyone. So, I rationalized this and decided that if I were unlovable (which I thought I was), any relationship I engaged in would end poorly.

Platonic relationships.
Romantic relationships.
Mentoring relationships.
Familial relationships.

They would all end tragically...
So why even try?

This was yet another unhealthy trauma response. While I was in the middle of the hurt, I viewed it as something that was justified. Something that I *had* to do to survive. Looking back, I can now see where this was a toxic behavior I learned from those who abused me.

The cutting people off once they realized "what I was really like." Always trying to present a picture-perfect image and never allowing myself to be vulnerable. Never admitting when I was at fault. Constantly viewing myself as the victim. Demonizing everyone around me because I thought I couldn't trust them.

I learned these behaviors from those who hurt me.

I viewed myself as the victim,
but I didn't realize I was developing
the characteristics of the villain.

We learn toxic behaviors, coping mechanisms, and traits when we grow up in a harmful environment. We can find ourselves modeling the behavior being directed at us. Sometimes it's intentional, and we want to inflict the pain that has been inflicted on us onto someone else. Other times (and most times), it isn't intentional; we aren't cognizant of what we are doing.

It flies under our radar, so it may take years to notice. Sometimes it even takes an outsider calling us out on it for us to even notice. Harrison has always (gently and lovingly) called me out on things that were clearly an unhealthy coping mechanism I developed. When others point this out to you, it's best to not get defensive (a common coping mechanism) because they are doing it out of love. And in the long run, it will benefit you... even if the truth stings at first.

The truth of the matter is that it is our responsibility to unlearn these toxic traits and behaviors so that we don't perpetuate the cycle of abuse. No one else can do it for us. It is a lot of work. It's hard. Unlearning these things can be painful at times, but it is healthy *at all times*.

We all like to talk about the first few steps of trauma recovery and immediately jump to the end when living outside of our brokenness. We want to skip over the hard part -- the work involved in moving on.

Unlearning behaviors that are not healthy for us is a big step. Instead of refusing to acknowledge that there is something in us that needs to change, being honest with ourselves is vital. Unlearning these things requires consistency... you can't erase years of experience overnight.

We need to be able to put in the work to change our behavior. It requires consistency. The harsh truth is that sometimes we can be blind to our own bitterness and resentment because we've been excusing (and therefore disguising) our own unhealthy behavior.

The biggest thing I have had to fight in my life was using my trauma as a crutch. Whenever something went wrong, I would instantly blame it on my childhood. If I'm being honest, I used my trauma to escape blame as a teenager. I was constantly living in a victim's mindset. I thought everyone was always out to get me.

I was also guilty of always being on the defense. I was always ready to defend myself against everyone... anyone. I would always keep everyone an arm's length away from me.

This unfair behavior was even directed at Harrison for almost the entire beginning years of our relationship. We got married on our fifth anniversary of being together (a year and a half spent being engaged). For the first two years of our relationship... bless his heart... I treated Harrison with suspicion, lacked trust in him, and constantly doubted that he was as good as he appeared. He was too good to be true to me.

I was projecting my experiences with other people onto him. It was utterly unfair to him; he had done nothing to cause this behavior. In fact, Harrison did many things to disprove this suspicion I held against him. This was unfair, unhealthy behavior... but at the time... I thought I was justified.

I thought that since I was doing this for the purpose of self-preservation, it made it okay. In reality, it was wrong. Harrison was the opposite of what I had experienced, yet I still held that against him.

It was up to me to change this pattern of behavior. It was up to me to allow God to heal my mindset. It was up to me to embrace the work that He was trying to do in my mind. At the end of the day, it was my responsibility to work on it.

We often find ourselves needing to unlearn unhealthy responses to trauma. But sometimes, we don't just need to unlearn the things *that we do* that are negative. Sometimes we need to unlearn the things that were done and said to us. For the longest time, I believed that my life was meaningless, and I was a waste of valuable space.

I was held captive by my own mind. The people who had abused me poisoned my mind. I thought there was no point in continuing to live because I would never be able to amount to anything -- never able to make a difference.

Unlearning. One of the biggest lessons I've had to learn about recovering from something traumatic... unlearning... something I'm still working on to this day.

Unlearning attitudes I saw and copied.
Unlearning unhealthy coping mechanisms I developed
because I thought I wouldn't survive without them.
Unlearning the rejection.
Unlearning normalizing the things done to me.
Unlearning the horrible words directed at me.
The names. The threats. The lies.

But through God…
my saving strength.

He's been there every step of the way. He's strengthened me. Guided me. Loved me. He gives healing to the hurt. He can do the same for you.

CHAPTER SEVENTEEN:
Let God Use You As He Sees Fit

*"But **the fruit of the Spirit** is love, joy, peace,*
longsuffering, gentleness, goodness, faith,
meekness, temperance: against such there is no law."
— Galatians 5:22-23 (KJV)

As I write this chapter, I am sitting in my home. My home. A word that I wanted to be able to say for so long. All I wanted was a home... a place where I could feel safe and like I belonged. Home. I still can't get over that word.

A home I share with my husband. Another word I can't get over. I have a fur-baby that clutters that home, but I don't mind. I am living the prayers I cried myself to sleep muttering. I am living the prayers I prayed during the darkest times of my life. God was with me every step of the way. Even when I couldn't see it.

This is my journey to joy.
A joy unspeakable.

Our journeys might not look the same, but that's okay.
They all end the same way... with Jesus.

I'm still on my journey. There is still a lot for me to learn. No matter how educated or experienced you think you are, there is always more to learn. I still have so much to experience. I still have much more to learn about myself, life, and living beyond the hurt.

There are still things that I have to unlearn. I still must work on some negative core beliefs that I haven't fully worked through. Because I grew up in a house that was not safe, I still sometimes view the world as unsafe. I still take extra precautions that a person who hasn't experienced might not take to feel a sense of safety.

The goal of writing this book wasn't to make me out as the poster child for learning to move on from past trauma and forgive when it seems impossible. In fact, I messed up a lot along the way. Sharing our testimonies builds the faith of others. It helps remind them that God is capable of rescuing them when they forget. It reminds others that no obstacle can stand in His way. That's the goal of this book. To glorify God for turning what seemed like ruins into a whole new beautiful landscape.

The last lesson from my season of restoration I want to leave with you is this: you don't have to wait until you are fully "recovered" to let God use you to bring light to His saving power. You can tell your story… even while it's still unfolding. I thought I needed to be fully recovered and whole before I was able to answer God's call for me.

For example, if I were called to be a Sunday school teacher…. I thought I had to wait until I was whole to start volunteering in the nursery, assisting teachers in their classes, or offering to buy snacks for the Sunday School kids. I thought that I needed to wait to do anything while I was still recovering.

Or if I were called to be a missionary to a specific country…. I thought that I had to wait until I was fully recovered to start learning the language spoken in that country, researching the country's history, and reaching out to people who have connections to that country to learn more. I thought I needed to wait to prepare until I was whole.

In Genesis, you see the story of Joseph (Genesis 37:1-Genesis 50:26). If you aren't familiar with Joseph, he was the son of Israel (formerly called Jacob) and Rachel. He had eleven (named and known) brothers and one (named and known) sister. He was his father's favorite, which was very apparent from the start. There was no denying that Joseph was the preferred child.

As a result, Joseph's brothers became very jealous and bitter. To summarize this story, it all came to a head when that favoritism was symbolized in the form of a coat. His father gave him a coat of many colors; no record in the Bible shows the brothers getting even a boring-looking coat specially gifted to them by their father.

Many people, when telling this story, make the brothers out to be these unrelatable monsters who sold Joseph into slavery for no reason. People who were completely inhumane with absolutely zero redeeming qualities. I think the reality is that we can all find ourselves looking like the brothers from time to time. Sometimes they are a little too relatable... and we don't want to admit that.

This one act sets the stage for more traumatic experiences for Joseph... being falsely accused of sexual assault, being thrown in prison, being forgotten in prison, and being separated from everything he knew throughout the whole time. Not to mention any potential physical and emotional abuse he experienced during that time as well.

Eventually... Joseph is finally remembered and let out of prison. In fact, he became the second most powerful person (aside from Pharoah) in Egypt. During this time of restoration... after he met and forgave his brothers... after (by God's lead) he saved Egypt... he had children. Two, to be exact.

In Genesis 41:52, Joseph named one of his sons Ephraim because...

*"God hath caused me to be **fruitful** in the **land of my affliction.**" (KJV)*

Ephraim ['Ephrayim -- Strong's Number: 0669] means "fruitful." Joseph acknowledged that even in his darkest times, there was still hope. In a different sense of the word "fruitful," we should still live with a purpose even when going through trials, just like Joseph did.

We should still try to love others when we feel unloved. We should still strive to help others find peace and joy when it is lacking in our lives. We should still bear the Fruit of the Spirit when everything seems to be spiraling out of control.

It is possible to be fruitful during times of heaviness. It is possible to be fruitful during times that you want to forget. We can be patient. We can still show love. We can still have joy. We can still experience peace. We can still exercise long-suffering. We can still remain gentle. We can still strive for goodness. We can still have that anchor of faith. We can still be meek.

We can still allow God to use us wherever He sees fit while we recover. We can still minister to the broken and hurting while we are broken and hurting. That gives us an understanding of what they are going through. It creates a connection point.

I don't know what lies ahead; I'm not the author of my story. But regardless of what may come my way, I know the Author. I trust the Author. For the first time in my life, I can finally say that I truly have joy. It's the same joy that is promised to us all.

My journey to joy didn't go as planned…
but I wouldn't have it any other way.
I'm still learning to live beyond the brokenness
that surrounded me.

Beyond the pain.
Beyond the ruins of addiction.
Beyond the betrayal of abuse.

I'm still learning to live beyond the hurt -- and that's okay. I'm a work in progress; we all are! I don't want to live to see a day where God is no longer working in me and through me. Let Him do a work in you… one only He is capable of.

Allow Him to use you… your story… as He sees fit. When He does, remember that it's for His glory… not ours. Remember to be humble and exalt Him above yourself.

And lastly… always remember that there is healing found in His name.

www.ingramcontent.com/pod-product-compliance
Lightning Source LLC
Chambersburg PA
CBHW070807280326
41934CB00012B/3092